WISDOM AND FOLLY IN RELIGION

WISDOM AND FOLLY IN RELIGION

A STUDY IN CHASTENED PROTESTANTISM

BY

Joseph Haroutunian

PRESBYTERIAN THEOLOGICAL SEMINARY,
CHICAGO

WIPF & STOCK · Eugene, Oregon

Wipf and Stock Publishers
199 W 8th Ave, Suite 3
Eugene, OR 97401

Wisdom and Folly in Religion
A Study in Chastened Protestantism
By Haroutunian, Joseph

ISBN 13: 978-1-60899-006-1
Publication date 8/31/2013
Previously published by C. Scribner's Sons, 1940

DEDICATED WITH AFFECTION AND GRATITUDE

TO

MY FORMER COLLEAGUES AND STUDENTS

AT

WELLESLEY COLLEGE

INTRODUCTION

This book speaks so directly to our condition that it needs little introduction. It is addressed to all who have been unable to escape the tragic sense of life, to all who contemplate with fear and pity the lot of suffering, sinful man on the torn earth, to all wrestlers with God. It speaks to and it confirms our doubt in the efficacy of religion to save us from disaster; it is almost exuberantly iconoclastic in its attack on modern superstitions. It honors the honesty of those who do not want to fool themselves with wishful thinking about beneficent deities who seek nothing but human happiness. It makes no effort to justify the ways of God to man.

But Professor Haroutunian's iconoclasm is deeply religious. His anti-religion is like that of the prophets and his protest against contemporary religion is like that of the early Protestants. If he attacks the fallacies of self-determinism he does so in the name of divine and not of economic determinism; if he pours scorn on man's effort to defend his sense of central importance in the world he does so in the name of God's glory and not in the name of meaninglessness and chance. Perhaps it is quite wrong to call so much attention to the polemical tendencies in these chapters; the note of assurance, the confession of faith in divine sovereignty and in the forgiveness of sins are more moving and fundamental elements. As one proceeds from page to page these themes rise up in ever stronger volume and in ever new variations.

The writer has gone far toward the accomplishment of two tasks which are but one for him. The first of these is the effort to make explicit and to interpret in Christian terms the implicit religious content of the modern mind. By the modern mind Professor Haroutunian does not mean the nineteenth-century mind which gloried in man's conquest over nature and denied the teachings of science by making a religion of science. He means the mind of the twentieth century which has been sadly disappointed with the gospel of self-salvation and has learned from science as from politics how little the world is subject to the wishes of men. Professor Haroutunian has a deep sympathy for the apparent atheism of that mind; beneath the atheism he discerns a cosmic orientation and a realistic understanding for man's plight in the world. The second task is that of stating afresh the faith of the Reformers which modern Protestantism sets forth in pale images when it does not pervert it. Luther, Calvin and Edwards—read with a humble desire to understand their meaning rather than with a sense of superiority—have illuminated for the author the state of every man in need of God. In them he has found that resolute facing of the hard and unpalatable facts about man and God which the twentieth-century mind demands. So he brings the sixteenth and twentieth centuries together. His new Protestantism is both older than the Reformation, since it draws its inspiration from the same Biblical source the Reformers used, and younger than that revolution, since it is born out of the conditions of the present age.

Such work is of the greatest importance. Whether we think of democracy or of the Church or of what is more important than either, the soul of the individual man in the confusions of our time, it becomes increasingly evident that deeper foundations of conviction and principle than we have been accustomed to use are required if we are not to be confounded. That democracy, the Church and the individual soul in fact are more deeply founded in a more ultimate faith than we have assumed is becoming ever more evident. To make explicit what has been implicit, to penetrate through our history to the foundations which underlie our history is an inescapable task of our time. One must be deeply grateful for a book which advances this work so much as *Wisdom and Folly in Religion* does, for a book, moreover, which does not "smell of the study" but is the evident product of inner struggles and human sympathies.

H. Richard Niebuhr.

ACKNOWLEDGMENTS

I am deeply grateful to Professor Louise P. Smith of Wellesley College for her constant encouragement and help, without which I would have been unable to write and finish this little book. She has been most generous with her time and effort, with her criticisms and suggestions which I have utilized throughout my work. I am heavily indebted to Professor Herbert W. Schneider of Columbia University for his painstaking work towards the improvement of the form and content of this book, and for the friendly encouragement he has offered me at all times. My hearty thanks are due to Professor H. Richard Niebuhr of Yale University for many important suggestions and for the indispensable Introduction he has contributed. I am grateful to Professor Muriel S. Curtis for several helpful criticisms, and to Mr. William L. Savage of Charles Scribner's Sons who has been a ready and generous helper in the preparation of this book for the press.

I have nothing to say in apology or explanation for the following pages. I have stated the truth as I have seen it. Yet I offer no ready-made truth, for the pleasure and satisfaction of any one. Truth for each man has to be wrought in his own soul, revealed by God and through much labor and pain. I trust, however, that God will make the reading of this book an occasion for reflection and edification, for the increase of wisdom and love among us.

J. H.

CONTENTS

III

ON THE PROBLEM OF RIGHTEOUSNESS

Chapter One

GOD ALONE IS GOD

1. Protestantism in Our Time
2. Justification by God
3. Justification Otherwise
4. The Kinship of Protestantism and Contemporary Unbelief

1. *Protestantism in Our Time*

IN A WORLD wherein man's perennial and evidently chronic inhumanity to man has assumed monstrous proportions and become, in the words of the prophet Isaiah, an "overflowing scourge," the futility of religion has become scandalous and deeply disquieting. Our world has become a whirlpool of sin and suffering. Millions of men live in fear and insecurity. Multitudes are engaged in a pathetic struggle for existence, without offering so much as a passing tribute to justice and kindness. Men come together to wield power and to coerce the powerful. Races are maligned, suppressed, and oppressed. And all live under the shadow of vast and sinister forces which threaten to turn the world into a devil's playground of rapine, tyranny, and murder. In the midst of this Babylon, the Church, "the City of God," stands, rather sits, disabled and stripped of both visible and invisible glory. Indeed she prays for justice and peace; but the Lord will not hear her because of her many sins and the folly of her ways in this her pilgrimage in Babylon; because her love of God is become cold and because she has learned to play the harlot with the gods of the nations. She prays. But her hands are unclean, her heart divided and her mind confused. Therefore her goodness is become as the morning dew, and her power as that of flesh.

This is certainly the case with the churches called Protestant and their religion with which this essay is mainly concerned. It is hard to imagine anything more pathetic than the vanity of "religion" in our present common life. Our numerous churches, with their imposing externals, their multitudes of ministers and members, their vast incomes and spendings, their continued activities, their preaching and sociabilities, constitute in fact a negligible factor in the formation of our social life and destiny. The people continue their buying and selling; they patronize the theatres and music halls; they congregate in fields of sport; they cast their votes in favor of party or candidate—all without the benefit of religion. The beliefs promulgated and professed in the churches have the vaguest relevance to business, politics, education, the arts and the sports, all of which occupy almost all of the time and interest of the people. Our common morality is conditioned by the necessities of the several activities of our life together. The principles of fair play, prudence, decency, and good taste which govern our daily conduct, have no genuine kinship with "the principles of Jesus" pronounced from our pulpits. Our actual morality has its roots in the common desire to live happily and well. We attend to the "ethics of Jesus" on Sunday mornings because thus we are enabled to pay verbal tribute to high ideals, and we tolerate it because it fails to contradict the lower actualities of daily life. The ethical message of Protestantism has become utterly ambiguous. It remains an ineffective antidote to the widespread strife and suffering generated by our common and respectable preoccupation with the goods of the world and our enjoyment of them.

The Protestant churches seem to continue their existence mainly by virtue of their past, because they already are a part of community life and provide for a measure of social intercourse established by habit. The Sunday morning service, ladies' and young people's groups, bazaars and picnics, contribute to community cohesion and give people a sense of social importance and security. The charitable activities of the churches are useful exercises in mild benevolence and enhance the self-esteem of the donors. However, such values in religion do not make it a serious and important matter, and cannot dispel the fear that Protestantism has lost its character and its essential function in society.

Protestant thought of today is a religious version of the mind of our age, especially in its humanistic aspects. Its heart is set upon the improvement and happiness of man. Hence, its essential doctrines are the supreme worth of men and of human ideals such as peace and mutuality, men's ability to achieve virtue and happiness, and their innate and effective inclination towards the exercise of such power. Its cogitations on Christian truth are conditioned by these convictions. The love of God for man is justified by the "infinite value of human personality." When Jesus is praised as "divine," it is made clear that He is such by virtue of His "perfect humanity." The ideal of a painless world has become essential to the conception of the Kingdom of God. Our moralists prefer love and service to suffering of body and soul as essentials of the Christian way of life. Such humanitarianism is presented as evangelical, but few care if it is truly Protestant.

Furthermore, the Protestant mind of today consists of fragments of the historic Christian theology, so thrown together as to make a caricature of both Catholicism and Protestantism: God the Father Almighty has become God the Father; Jesus Christ, God Incarnate, has become a godlike man; the Holy Spirit is now an inward operation of God with dubious reality of His own. Man is a child of God, although not by adoption; he is capable of goodness, which hardly implies that he is now a sinner. The Church is a community of men who seek to love God and especially their neighbor, and an institution dedicated to the promotion of idealism and spirituality; it is no longer a community of God's elect. Baptism initiates the child into the Christian fold, but does not alter his inheritance from Adam. The Lord's Supper is intended as a reminder of Jesus' love and death, and nourishes the soul as the partaker of it is moved by his own reflections and sentiments. Good works inspired by love are necessary for goodness, but the absence of them does not signify eternal damnation.

Such fragmentary and innocuous Catholicism is often justified as "New Testament religion": This is hardly necessary. For, although one is happy to profess a religion with scriptural support, it is no longer expected that one be bound by the ideas of any given evangelist or apostle. In fact, the Gospels have become problems, and the Epistles are interesting as source books for the student of the evolution of early Christianity. Their unity and authority having become very doubtful, they allow any one to extract from them, or read into them, the religion which seems most satisfactory. Therefore, naturally enough, the Scriptures have become a multitude of texts which serve as starters for Sunday-morning perorations on the good life. Nobody cares much whether such "sermons" are scriptural, Protestant, Catholic, or simply moralistic. It is enough that they should be "Christian," inspiring, agreeable, and platitudinous.

The Protestants have ceased to believe that there is a Protestant mind worthy of serious consideration. The erstwhile popular principles of Protestantism, such as its devotion to the Bible as against "Popery," its anti-sacerdotalism, its passion for "the liberty of conscience," have become dead issues and no longer inspire enthusiasm. Now that the conflict with the Papacy has subsided, the Protestants have lost all interest in "the Reformation principles," and prefer to live without the benefit of the insights of the Reformers into the Christian religion. Indeed, few are those who care to turn to the latter for inspiration and instruction in the search for light in this our day of intellectual and moral perplexity. The very mention of "justification by faith," or of "the sovereignty of God," or of "election and predestination," or of the Bible as "the Word of God," are sufficient to confound enlightened Protestants with shame and to cause immediate and vehement protestations of utter disdain for such benighted and "unchristian doctrines." Even where ignorance and contempt for truth do not hold such limitless sway, such characteristic Protestant ideas (for the Protestant reinterpretations of them have been radical) are restated in conformity with the tastes of our "enlightened age." The sovereignty of God is so interpreted as to make certain that no shadow of doubt is cast upon the sovereignty of man. Justification by faith has become second to justification by works of love. Election and predestination are replaced by ideas of a divine love which will never permit itself to compromise our freedom to will good or evil. The authority of the Bible has become palatable in the sense that it somehow provides unique stimuli for piety and good works.

Such Protestantism has lost its soul. Before it makes any significant contribution to the life of men in our time, it must be born again, into our own time and in a certain likeness to the Protestantism of the Reformation. The latter, we are convinced and will attempt to show in this essay, has a profound kinship with the spirit of the contemporary man, and may well inspire and instruct us towards a Protestantism which shall do justice both to the mind and to the need of our age. The discovery of this kinship may well become an occasion for the infusion of new power into contemporary Protestantism, and make it something more than an opiate for some people. Under God, it may once again make the Protestant religion a leaven of righteousness in our midst. God is almighty, and able to deliver when we turn to Him ready to hear, to understand, and to obey. God's Word, spoken to those who come to Him in their own situation and need, ready to benefit from His Word to others who have listened to Him in *their* situation and need, is like "fire and like a hammer that breaketh the rocks to pieces." With this in mind, we turn to consider first the Protestant doctrine of "justification by faith," in the light of our own situation and need.

2. *Justification by God*

Medieval religion was a highly developed system of ideas and practices which provided men with "the means of grace," with a way of deliverance from sin, the devil, death, and hell. It offered them the ways and means whereby they could attain a clear conscience and enter into eternal life. Baptism was birth into the supernatural life. Penance was the means for effacing sins which endangered this new life. The Eucharistic Sacrifice was the supernatural food which nourished the soul of the baptized believer. Extreme Unction was the last exercise of the Church's power against sin and the devil. Those who sought maximum assurance of salvation were provided with rules and exercises in piety, leading to the "contemplative life." In mystic communion with God men enjoyed the foretaste of the Vision of God which is beyond sin and death.

In spite of all the theoretical precautions taken by theologians, the practical outcome of such religion was considerable control over God. In the name of God, the priesthood exorcised the devil, absolved sins, administered spiritual food, and dispatched the pious to heaven or purgatory. Thus they claimed to possess divine power and used it. The fine distinctions they made between their persons and their offices were insufficient to guard them against the superstition that *they* were able to give or withhold the "means of grace." Faith in God, in the Church, and in the priesthood, could hardly be distinguished one from another. The Church could not escape the temptation to declare that *if* the people believed and acted as prescribed, they would attain salvation. The idea of justification by works became a widespread and potent misconception.

Faith *and* love, under God, became causes of salvation, and the power of man to destroy sin and death became an accepted, even when not acknowledged, superstition. Thus under a thick covering of argument from reason and the Bible, religion and magic joined hands in mitigating man's sense of helplessness before his destiny and in providing him with the conviction that he is in possession of the Way, and the Truth, and the Life.

Religion is seldom free from magic. Men are perennially unwilling to acquiesce in the freedom and the sovereignty of the God or gods they worship. They are not satisfied to pray for rain, or for good crops, or for deliverance from their enemies, from sin and death. They pretend to be in possession of means and powers which will ensure for them the good they seek, which will constrain or coerce their God or gods to give them what they desire. They beat drums, dance, drink lotions, eat supernatural food, and do a multitude of "good works." Thus they guarantee their peace, prosperity, and even immortality. In such "religion" there is no clear congruity between means and ends, no genuine distinction between real and imaginary causes, no adequate sense of the limits of human power. Yea, man even flourishes weapons against sin and death, and turns his prayer into an instrument for coercing his God or gods into subservience to his will. In an atmosphere of mystery and confused ideas, credulity presents the supernatural as natural, the human as divine; and man learns to trust in his own deeds rather than in the power of the Deity. He achieves an illusory mastery over his environment, pretends to be upright and immortal, and lives happily believing that his destiny is in his own hands. Such "religion" often produces imposing apologies for its presumptions, rationalizes its overbeliefs with formidable arguments, confounds the mind and wins over the heart. Thus it becomes convincing and comforting to many, and attains great prestige among the people.

The Protestant doctrine of "justification by faith" was radical repudiation of a lie which religion ever generates: that "hocus-pocus" makes the impossible possible; that man can destroy his sin, or that he can raise himself from the dead. It replaced man where he belongs: in the world where past evil burdens the present and the future is given over to death. Thus it exposed the magic in the Christian religion, and rediscovered evangelical piety or faith. It established the truth that unless God save us, we are lost; that we live as sinners, die as sinners, and perish, unless Someone not man, Someone who is sovereign over the world and its courses, destroy our past and reconstitute our future. The wild and defiant scorn which Luther heaped upon "religion" in his day was the product of such single-eyed vision of the futility of man's efforts to shake off the burden of the past and to steal his way into eternal happiness. He made it impossible for true Protestants to acquiesce in the solemn self-deception of mysterious deeds whereby men seek to coerce the will of their god, to imprison the eternal in the temporal, to destroy sin and death; in short to become gods: both sinless and immortal. Such was one essential aspect of the Lutheran revolution in religion.

Justification by faith, Luther's formula for his revolutionary teaching, was not altogether felicitous. Man is not justified by faith. It is *God*, and not man's exercise of a virtue called faith, that justifies. Faith as an act of man is the last resource of magical religion. "Believe in God," says the medicine man within, "and you will be saved." "Trust in God," says the author of confusion, "and you will overcome your sin." "*Feel* God," he says, "and you are immortal." Such is the last stand of the Deceiver who would keep man in bondage to sin and death; who would poison man's heart and mind, and make him blind to the elemental truth of his humanity. Unable to make man trust the work of trust in himself, he lures him to trust the work of trust in God. Thus the devil triumphs again. A new foundation is laid for magic: a foundation which is much more vicious than all others. For now, the man who would be saved has only to think or feel something. He does not even have to *do* anything. And behold, he is saved! This is the last word in superstition, and harder than all others to eradicate, because it conceals itself under a solid coating of "faith in God." Thus originates the supreme folly of the man who thinks he is just because he has faith, yea who thinks his faith is justice. Plausible magic (wherein one seeks to fit the means to the end) is replaced by outrageous magic (wherein one seeks to coerce God by mere sentiment or a nod of the head). Such a doctrine of "justification by faith" is a perversion of Protestantism.

The early Protestant conception of "justification by faith" is a different matter. In spite of the confusions which crept into the mind of Luther, the ex-Augustinian monk, he was persistent in the conviction that the "righteousness of God" is the sole cause of man's justification. The rock underneath Protestantism is the "righteousness of God." To say that we are justified by faith is to say that God is righteous. To say that God is righteous is the same thing as to say that in Him is man's only hope of salvation. It is to say that God is love. To believe that God is love is to have faith. Faith does not justify; it says that God justifies. Faith does not make men righteous; it says that God is righteous. Faith *does* nothing; it *says* something: God is love.

Still, the devil will not give up. With a pious smile concealing a heart of boundless perfidy, he says, "God *justifies*. When you believe in God, you become just." See the depths of his malice! He would confound the Spirit in His labor and struggle against the sin in us. "Now you are just," he says; "the sin in you is dead. God be thanked, now you are a righteous man. You obey the commandments of God. You give alms, and pray, and fast. Look within! Do you not love God and your neighbor? Yea, even your enemies? Pray, do not be mistaken. You did not make yourself just. You were a helpless sinner, and God had mercy on you and justified you. It would be wicked to think otherwise. Nevertheless, now you are a lover of God and an upright man. Praise be to God!"

The Tempter is plainly lying. God does not so justify me that I am without sin. The war between the flesh and the Spirit is never at an end, except when the Spirit leaves the soul of man in horror and disgust. While the Spirit is with us, we can never say: "I love God and man as I ought. I give alms, and pray, and fast as I ought. Now I am just before God." Those who consider the righteousness of God become embarrassed. They know that they are not just. And they pray as they were taught: "Forgive us our debts as we forgive our debtors."

Man's justification is the triumph of the love of God. It marks the collapse of self-justification: of lying, hypocrisy, and delusion. It is the foundation of self-knowledge or humility. It is the token of our liberation from bondage to sin, rooted in our knowledge of the persistent and all-pervading sin in us. It does not turn us into gods; it teaches us to be men. It does not clothe us with angelic purity; it bestows the grace of repentance upon us; it humbles and chastens the sin in us. It does not make us upright; it justifies us. It delivers us from bondage to our sin, in so far as we learn to repent and forgive, to forgive and repent.

For men confronted with the perennial sin in themselves and in others, the dialectic of repentance and forgiveness is essential to sanity. "Forgive us our debts as we forgive our debtors." To know the sin within and around us is the first condition of evangelical charity. It is the foundation of that elusive "humanity" which we seek and seldom attain. It is our only hope for the kindness and love which strive against the pride and censoriousness within us. It marks our virtual deliverance from self-righteousness, from that destructive zeal for fashioning others after our own image, from the folly of loving our ideals better than the men around us, from the ultimate sin of spiritual domination over others. Knowledge of the sin within us is our true freedom as human beings. It is our justification.

Man is never so exposed to the wiles of the devil as when he is religious. There is no man who will not make his faith in God an occasion for self-satisfaction. No man gives alms, prays, and fasts without self-congratulation. No man loves virtue and hates wickedness without loving himself. No man lives virtuously without judging his neighbor. No man loves God, whom he fashions in his own image, without that pride which leads him to censure his fellow men who are not gods. No man can be recognized as religious without also being suspected of hypocrisy. Self-love, pride, hypocrisy increase with piety, and are sanctified through their union with it. Thus religion becomes a pretense and a scandal. It is not only the Cross of Christ that makes Christianity a stumblingblock to the children of this generation. Men often turn against "religion" because they perceive the vainglory attached to it, because they see in it an occasion for complacency and an obstacle to genuine mutual understanding among men. Charity among men is impossible without a perception of our sin and death which bind us together as sons of Adam. When men believe that they have found a way of escape from sin and death, they become blinded to the kinship of men to one another in their common need for God, who alone can forgive sins and raise the dead. Thus the roots of compassion in the human soul become weakened and dry, and self-love triumphs over understanding and love among men. The recognition of this fact was a constant motive behind Luther's harsh polemic against the monks of his day, "the religious" or "spiritual" who knew the way to God and walked upon it.

The doctrine of justification by faith marks the collapse of religion as a bridge to eternity. It is the final vindication of the truth concerning man: that he is a creature. It is the triumph of reason over superstition, of reality over a dream world, of fact over fancy. It is an act of ultimate courage whereby man looks at his place in the world without squinting and "seeing things." It is the courage to admit that we did not make the sun and cannot alter its course, the courage to recognize that we cannot destroy the past or decree our own destiny. It distinguishes religion from magic, faith from superstition, and piety from idolatry. It is the ultimate safeguard against the folly and pride which infest man's spiritual life and turn it into rebellion against God.

The principle of justification by faith is the truly Protestant answer to the common and resented charges of "wishful thinking," and "escape from reality." Our theologians and ministers continue to offer apologies for religion which are impotent against the cultivated and the uncultivated unbeliever in our time: "There are several things wrong with you. You do not have the right kind of experience. You do not realize that 'there is something of the divine in man.' You are not sufficiently impressed with the intimations of the Eternal which come through worship and prayer. You will not admit that the 'experience of the divine' points to a 'divine Object.' You might admit that such experience makes it at least probable that there is a God. . . . You are equally poor in judging the realities of the moral life. Is it not marvellous that we can distinguish between right and wrong, yea that we have a conscience which tells us that this is right and that is wrong. Is it not most probable that we have this faculty from God, that the voice of conscience is the voice of God? May it not be that your own moral blindness and wickedness keep you from the knowledge of God? *We* are so impressed by our conscience that we are sure it reveals God to us. There may be other ways of accounting for the moral sense; but *we* choose to think it reveals a 'moral government of the world'! . . . Or will you object that your reason makes you unbelievers? *We* find our reason most congenial to belief in God. We are not at all impressed with the arguments against going 'from nature to God.' The unity and continuity of nature, the evidences of design and purpose in it, its beauty and glory all around us, lead us to the excellent hypothesis that God is working in and through the universe known to science and common sense. Indeed, we are aware of the evils in the world. But we can get around them by conceiving God's power as limited both by nature and by the free will of man; which latter, by the way, we believe in no less than in God. . . . In fact, all your difficulties with religion are rooted in your lack of proper reverence for man: for his religious experience, his conscience, his reason, his free will. This is where all our differences originate. You do not believe in man, and we do. You are impressed by the wickedness of man; we, by his goodness. You emphasize his kinship with the beasts; we, his kinship with the angels (so to speak). You celebrate his struggle for existence; we, his willingness to sacrifice himself for the good of others.

In the stupidity and mortality of man, you see the beast; in his nobility and idealism we see his godlikeness and the seeds of his immortality. In short, in man you see sin and death; in him, we see righteousness and the promise of eternal life. . . . We shall not be so dogmatic as to say that we *know* we are right and you are wrong. But we do believe it. God help us!"

Such Protestantism is a plain perversion of the truth which underlay the Reformation; namely, that man *needs* God. Luther saw through the pretensions of reason, religion, conscience, and free will. With an adroitness given only to those who are at once very wise and very simple, he struck at the root of human evil: the pretense that man is a god. He thus exposed the folly of reason, the faithlessness of religion, the hypocrisy of conscience and the bondage of "free will." He saw that nothing in man can save him from sin and death. And upon this rock he founded the Protestant faith.

Protestantism has no quarrel with reason which reveals man's true humanity, with conscience which reveals man's actual disobedience to God's Law, with "free will" which establishes man's responsibility for his acts. Such reason, conscience, and free will are essential to our humanity, and enjoy the status of facts. The Lutheran protest against them was inspired by the common prostitution of them in the interests of human self-deification. Men's unwillingness to live by their faith in God has always tempted them to live by the illusion that by reason they know God, by conscience they obey, or even possess God, and by the power of their will they can attain the eternal righteousness of God. To the Protestant who shares the insights of Luther and of the contemporary man, such use of reason, conscience, and "free will" is an abuse of them; it is a new version of the magic and idolatry which have always infested "natural piety."

Our Protestantism is partly a halfhearted reversion to the Catholic faith in man and in the works of man. The common appeal to spirituality and conscience as evidences of the divine in the human is a partial recovery of Catholic "fund of merit." If we want a religion which confuses the human and the divine, which makes pretensions for reason and conscience, and ends with a demand for the exercise of the "will to believe," which will give us techniques towards spiritual inebriation, which will rationalize our wishes and put our consciences to occasional or frequent sleep—then we had better forget Luther. If we want to find ways whereby we can institutionalize divine forgiveness and work our way into eternal life, then we had better keep away from "Reformation theology." If we want to control and use "means of grace" which will turn us into gods, or at least saints, then let us have none of "justification by faith." If we would trust our spirituality rather than God, it were better to return to Catholicism which can teach us both how to increase it and how to improve it. A Protestantism which survives as a pale and broken shadow of Catholicism has lost its reason for existence. For a while it will go on with its pious liturgies, dishonest "orthodoxy," vague and inane moralism, and its ludicrous bid for power in society. Then, it will either become truly Catholic or die in disgrace.

Protestantism and Catholicism will not mix. According to the latter, God Incarnate founded the Church, invested it with the keys to heaven and hell, gave it authority to teach supernatural truth embodied in its philosophical and moral theology, and made it the permanent repository of divine grace or power dispensed through the sacraments and actualized in miracles of healing, forgiveness, and the graded riches of supernatural life in the Church. It is rich in its hierarchical and monastic orders, in the world-wide distribution of its faithful who believe and obey their priests and bishops, in the co-ordinated and tremendous power it can exercise in the social and political decisions of its people. It is a treasure house of highest wisdom accumulated through the labors of generations of devoted and intelligent teachers. It has all the answers to the problems of life and destiny: whole, correct, and effective. It is a truly one, great, splendid, wise, and virtuous Church. Hence the Catholics resist the light-headed even though generous attempts of the Protestants to lure them into their conferences and to join hands over ambiguous generalities which are supposed to be the essentials of the Christian faith and practice.

Compared with Catholicism, Protestantism is poverty itself. The Protestant churches do not dispense supernatural virtues. They possess no Divine substance which forgives sins and raises the dead; they know of no infusions which transubstantiate man, turning a sinner into a saint, giving him a food which nourishes into holiness, and guarantees beatific vision, under well-defined and proper circumstances. They cannot offer men psychological certainty that there is a God who has given them a sure way to righteousness and resurrection from the dead. They have no authority to declare God's will and promises, and to bestow God's rewards upon the virtuous. They have no self-evident and unquestionable premises upon which they can build, consistently and logically, a true and complete system of moral and speculative theology; they do not possess "God's own Truth." They have no priesthood which can, in all seriousness and solemnity, offer the people the answer to the problem of sin-death, and prescribe the way to attain holiness-eternal life. They are divided in mind and body. Their people are scattered hither and thither, like sheep without a shepherd. They are schismatic, heretical, sinful, and lost. They do not possess God. They *need* Him.

3. *Justification Otherwise*

Alas, Protestantism has been unhappy with its need and its faith. It is very difficult to live in want while one's neighbor is enjoying his riches, to be a sinner while another is basking in the sun of "the Spiritual life," to lack the Truth and the Way while another has them both in full measure. Hence the vision of a powerful and prosperous Protestantism presents the Protestants with temptations which are well-nigh irresistible. *We* too must have the Truth, the Way, and the Life!

An uneasy Protestantism is sorely tempted to become dogmatic. The resurgence of a passion for believing the greatest number of traditional doctrines is often camouflaged as return to the essentials of Christianity. "We have ceased to be Christians. We do not believe the Creeds. We *must* believe them. Christianity is faith; it is belief. 'God so loved the world. . . .' If we are to be Christians we must believe the historic doctrines of the Creation, the Fall, the Preparation, the Incarnation, the Atonement, the Church, the Forgiveness of Sins, and the Resurrection of the Dead."

Now, such reversion to dogmatism is a futile gesture where there is no authoritarian church which demands and receives assent. There is no one in Protestantism who can impose upon another the duty of believing the Gospel. Belief in Protestantism is not a matter of obligation; it is an eager hearing of "the Gospel of God."

"God so loved the world . . ." is news. Nobody is bound to believe it. For a Protestant it is folly to think that believing the Gospel is a "good work." When one believes he acquires no virtue, no claim upon a reward, no means of entering into "eternal life." Believing or not believing will die with the believer or unbeliever. Even the most exalted or truthful belief perishes with him who believes it. To think otherwise is to believe in magic, however subtle or rarefied. The Protestant believes in God, and not in his belief. He receives the Gospel with joy: not because his receiving it saves him, but because God, in the Gospel, declares Himself his Savior. Protestantism is founded upon faith in God, and not upon assent to divine authority delegated to men. Where there is faith, there is also assent to the Gospel and its doctrines. Where there is no faith, Protestantism can do no more than preach the Word of God. Hence, it is futile for Protestants to taunt each other into "Christian belief." Dogmatism without authoritarianism, and authoritarianism without ecclesiastical orders, are mere caricatures of Catholicism.

Protestants who cannot believe are sorely tempted to "go practical." Thus we get a second travesty of Catholicism: justification by works. Protestantism began believing in justification by faith, without works. Now it believes in justification by works, without faith! "Love, love, love alone matters! What you believe, rather what you do not believe, is your own private affair. But love you *must*. Love yourself. Love your neighbor. Love your enemy. Love all mankind! By love are you saved. God is love. Love is God. Love is the only sure way to life eternal. You are justified by love and by the works of love!" Love is the best beloved idol in Protestantism, and "the way of love," the favorite magic in it. Love can do everything. It can destroy all sin. It can stop wars and oppressions. It can "bring in the Kingdom of God!" Such is the Protestant's crown of folly. Compared with it, the Catholic's principle of "faith and works" is wisdom, sobriety, and modesty. For the latter knows what discipline of body and soul, what prolonged "religious exercise," what ascetic rigor, go into the making of even a semblance of "holy love." But not so the Protestant! He is *born* with a generous supply of love! He only needs to be preached at occasionally, and he will proceed to love the total "race of mankind."

If faith dies with the believer, so does love die with the lover. There may be "immortal love," but this is neither my love nor that of any one else. It is indeed hard to believe so, for we love our love as we love no one. "Love is the best thing we have. If *it* also is mortal, then what hope have we? . . ." *We* have no ground for hope in us. When the Protestant reformers renounced the doctrine of merits, they left man with absolutely nothing in heaven or on earth with which he could justify himself. His love was no exception. Yea, this his most precious possession, which is the source of all good works and merits, was the object of their most violent and relentless attack. Protestants who "believe in love" are playing with a perverted Catholicism, and are the worst enemies of the Protestant faith. They have made us the laughing stock of the world. Men oppress and starve one another, complacent parasites live upon the labor of others, one race destroys another, and nations tremble with mortal fear of each other—while every Sunday morning thousands of Protestant ministers discourse pointlessly and harmlessly about the "greatest thing in the world." "Better than nothing?" Nay, worse than nothing. It is worse than nothing to put multitudes of sinners into a state of coma wherein they can no longer tell God's love from their sin. Worse idolatry and worse magic the world may have never known, for hardly ever before did men enter the Kingdom of God so easily!

Protestants whose belief is not faith and whose charity is not love have still another way of self-justification: They go to "worship services"! It is not necessary that God be central in worship, or that He be more than a brightish blur, an essence without life, mind, or even existence! Thousands flock to "worship services" in which they neither confess their sins nor fear Divine punishment, neither repent nor pray for forgiveness. Unaware of any radical insufficiency in themselves, equipped with a wish that they be a little better and happier, they seek in the "communion of saints" a painless stimulation towards some sort of pleasant spirituality and revindicate themselves in their own eyes and in the midst of a like-minded people. Thus they seek to arouse their emotions and to receive added power to be good and to do good, within well-defined limits dictated by common sense. The quest for direct visual and auditory stimuli, requiring minimum belief in "the living God," makes the usual Protestant service of hymn-singing, Scripture-reading, praying, and sermonizing quite unsatisfactory. These ordinary elements of the traditional Protestant church service require attention, understanding, and conviction. "*We* want to *feel religious.* We want a technique of worship which will give us spiritual experience without disturbing our minds or our consciences too much. We are now trying to work out set prayers, chanted responses and the like which, once one gets used to them, are inspiring without making undue demands upon one's credulity and thinking faculty. Somehow, mere repetition seems to make them spiritually effective: which is what we want. Besides, we are learning a great deal from Catholicism. We are getting used to the quartette choir and its imitation of plain song. Our choir is almost professional! You should hear them chant 'Praise ye the Lord.' 'Lord have mercy upon us,' all sorts of long Amens, and the like. Really, they are quite impressive. The responsive singing is not as good as it might be as yet; but the minister and the choir-leader are working on it: you know, the kind where the minister says something and the choir breaks into a moan in four parts; one line from the minister and one line from the choir, back and forth about a dozen times. The whole thing keeps one from falling asleep, and sometimes gives one a feeling of mystic drowsiness. It is restful and pleasant, and rather different from going to the movies. It gives one a sort of 'spiritual uplift,' and makes one wonder if there be not something behind it. . . . The stained glass windows with those antique Christs, apostles and saints, the gilded cross and would-be altar in front, the flowers sitting bashfully wherever they are placed—it all helps! It gives one a real feeling of a sort. The minister says that's 'the presence of ultimate Reality.' . . . He is really a very fine man: so decent, so eager, so kind, so inspiring; he is a real Christian. He preaches well, about love, beauty, patience, forgiveness, Jesus Christ, spiritual life, and the like. Once in a while he scolds us for our own good. But he doesn't overdo it. We don't mind it a bit. Besides, he prays beautifully. He can give you a real feeling of worship. . . . The 'Communion service'? Well, we have it about half a dozen times a year, oftener than formerly, and more sanitary. One is supposed to think of Jesus, which is always a good thing. I confess, though, I am completely lost when our minister takes up the plate of bread and says, 'Is not this my body, broken for you?' and when he takes the cup and says, 'Is not this my blood of the covenant shed for you?' (I may not be quoting him exactly.) Besides he says it all in such a strange tone; it sounds symbolical to me. I wonder if he really means it. Just the same though, he creates quite an atmosphere. . . . He says worship raises the tone of our lives. He thinks it makes us better Christians. I hope so. But honestly, I don't think it makes much difference."

"Worship" without our fear or faith is the ultimate symptom of Protestant degeneracy. When men come to church neither to confess their sins nor to hear God's Word of judgment and mercy, neither to hear God's Law nor to hear of His grace in Christ Jesus, neither to voice the cry of this body of sin and death nor to declare their hope by faith in Him who raised Jesus from the dead, in short when they come to church without their sin and go without forgiveness,—they turn worship into vanity, and religion into a spiritual farce. Protestant worship is the cry of the soul for deliverance from sin and death. It is directed towards the living God who alone is the Lord of righteousness and life. It is the Word of the same God who speaks in judgment and mercy, who creates the faith and hope in us, who struggles with the sin and death in us, commending His love towards us in Christ Jesus and teaching us to worship Him in spirit and in truth. We worship because we need God, because we believe in Him, because we hope in Him. We know what we need, what we believe, and what we hope. As we need, believe, and hope, so also we *feel*, and we worship. We cannot feel properly, worship properly, when we do not know our need and our hope. Worship in which "spiritual experience" replaces the need for deliverance from sin and death, and the faith and hope which go with it, is a stupid travesty of Protestantism. No man of sense can take it seriously; no such man does. Hence a Protestantism set to cultivate a species of esthetic enjoyment in the place of "the fear of God" has no Gospel for our generation.

4. *The Kinship of Protestantism and Contemporary Unbelief*

The Protestantism of our day is casting aside its opportunity to become a truly contemporary religion. Its "modernism" was a step in the proper direction. It struggled against the perversity of a religion (Fundamentalism) which simply repudiated the insights of the modern man, especially those connected with "science." It tried to adjust Protestantism to a conception of the world which revealed the medieval cosmogony of Fundamentalism as plainly false. It did away with the superstition that salvation depends upon assent to that which seems to be untrue. But "modernism" has lost its nerve. When "science and evolution," which it adopted with much noise and celebration, turned "naturalistic," when the latter discarded God and jeopardized "faith in man," the modernist Protestants forgot their quarrel with Fundamentalism, and in the name of "the infinite value of personality," set their eloquence against the pessimism and cynicism of the contemporary mind, for which "science" was at least partly responsible. The more the modern man woke up to the "dilemma of man in nature," the more he realized the power of the flesh and the ubiquity of evil in the world, the more he despaired in the presence of conflict and waste, both in man and in nature, the more he learned about man's bondage to his past and the more clearly he discerned the veil of death thrown upon the face of man and beast, in short, the more the modern man understood the "tragedy of man," the more Protestant modernists shouted their praises of God and man, especially of man. Preaching became apologetics, defiant harangue and endless reiteration of palpable falsehoods,—or at best half-truths. Faith became a Sunday-morning wondering whether there really be a God, whether the teachings and example of Jesus be worth a man's second thought, whether man can really achieve integrity, and whether he may hope for "eternal life," in one sense or another. Christian convictions were turned into a series of sporadic doubts concerning the witness of reason and the senses. Once again, religion set itself against known fact and reasoned truth. It became turgid thinking mixed with vague desire and ill-founded hope. Many people acquiesced in it for want of something better; but of course they could not take it seriously enough to live by it. Thus confusion and lip service to religion became a prevalent Protestant phenomenon. Many who had sufficient intellectual and moral honesty, as well as force, turned away from "religion," and went their several ways: to cynicism, or stoicism, or "practical idealism," or one of several varieties of "nature mysticism." Many who remained in the churches for one reason or another, learned to think their own thoughts and to live their daily lives without the benefit of their professed religion.

The misfortune of the present futility of Protestantism becomes all the more heartbreaking when one considers that the contemporary mind is profoundly congenial to the Reformation religion, and greatly in need of it. The Great War and its aftermaths have given us striking evidence of the moral limitations under which we labor. We have become chastened with regard to our good intentions and their products of futile gestures towards peace and justice in the world. Our social and economic sufferings have prepared us for the increased understanding of our part in the evils around us. The more dramatic manifestations of sin in our public life have lent increased weight to the naturalist's skepticism concerning the power of our sublime thoughts and emotions to produce benevolence and beneficence sufficient to "make a difference." We have become strongly aware that our idealism and pretended regard for the happiness of mankind fail us when they are most needed. We have even learned to be reconciled to our willingness to participate in public sin which promotes our self-interest and gives us comfort and security while others live in constant fear of destitution. Our confirmed and persistent regard for our own happiness has made us suspicious of kindly emotions we entertain towards those whose interests do not happen to conflict with our own. We are no longer so confident of our goodness, no longer capable of blissful ignorance of our participation in public sin, no longer blind to the persistent issuing of self-love in selfishness, no longer willing to conceal the lust in us under heavy coatings of respectability. Once again, we have become aware of the sin in us, although we call it "human nature." We do not expect to find a way of turning ourselves into "paragons of virtue." *We* have no way of justifying ourselves.

We have removed the gilt from many of our idols. We are less willing to worship the works of our own hands. We will not put our trust in our principles, we will not indulge in idealistic orgies, we will not dream dreams and see visions. We expect no solution to the "human problem," no end to our sinning and no beginning of eternal life upon this earth. We see no heaven, in this world or anywhere else. We suspect any one who says: "Lo, here; lo, there." We do not know the way to God, and we do not know of any man who does. We are not aware of our justification, and we suspect any one who is. We have no sense or intuition of, or evidence for, our immortality; and we are deeply suspicious of those who believe they have. We know no rest or peace of conscience, except through fatigue and indifference; and we regard quizzically those who do. *We* know of no way of deifying ourselves; we have no key to the door of heaven; we wield no weapon which can destroy our past; we possess no power which can alter our death and destiny. *We* are men, not *God.*

Contemporary atheism is the opportunity of a genuinely Protestant religion. Yes, the roots of true Protestantism are to be found more often among the unbelievers of our day than among the "loyal churchmen." If the consciousness of sin and death is a true mark of a healthy conscience and a reflective mind, or of true religion, then we will do well to look for these among the cynics and pessimists of our time, that is among those who can believe neither in God nor in man. These are the "publicans and sinners" of today who will enter the Kingdom of God before the comfortable and complacent believers who administer or receive the innocuous religion in our churches. *These* people live in the valley of the shadow of sin and death. They do not trust reason or goodwill to usher them into the heavenly peace and happiness of the pious.

They can see nothing beyond this life of confusion of goods and evils. . . . They know of no "heavenly Father" who makes it His business to satisfy their desires and to supply them with their wants. They are aware that the world is not built around them, and that it is not committed to making them happy. They see themselves as allotted a brief existence in a vast and enduring world, and set themselves, in all honesty, to wrest all the "fun" they can from it. Possessed of an unprofessed and unpublished sense of the vanity of life, they proceed to "make the best of a bad situation." They abhor death, try to ignore it, and live in sin. They fight over the world's goods, envy their neighbors, hate their enemies, despise the weak and helpless, exploit the dumb and ignorant, defy or dissuade their consciences, and fill the world with sin and suffering.

What has Protestantism to say to atheism? Before it can say anything worth while, it will have to face it and understand it. There has been too much of combating it with deficient argument. Books have been written and sermons preached offering poor reasons for believing that there is a God, that man is all but an angel (at the bottom), that the human situation is neither too unhappy nor too hopeless, that evil is not conclusive evidence against the goodness of the cosmos, that we may become eternalized one way or another. The people have been harangued towards the love of man and God, scolded for their indifference to "spiritual values," cajoled into lip service to idealism, and threatened about the probable consequence of their iniquities. They have been moved to pious sentimentalism, persuaded to give to charity, and praised for their virtues. And now they are being challenged to believe "the Gospel," to accept the authority of the Bible, to develop a new reverence for the "Church," and to combat the evils of society. Yet, in all this, there is little understanding of the problem of the contemporary man: his struggle against death and his consequent sin.

If Protestantism is to take advantage of its opportunity and do its duty in our day, it has to identify itself with the people. It has to share their pessimism, agnosticism, cynicism, and ultimate despair before sin, death, and hell. It has once again to learn to eat and drink with "the people of the land," with the publicans and harlots of our day. It has to defend and not anathemize those who break the fast and pluck ears of grain on the Sabbath day. It has to have compassion upon the multitude who have lost their Shepherd, and have gone astray, every one to his own way. It has to open its arms to the prodigal sons of God, and dress the wounds of those bleeding to their death.

Protestantism cannot compete with Catholicism as a religion of dogma and assent, of authority and obedience, of ritual and mysticism. It cannot administer supernatural food to immortal souls. It cannot forgive sins and perform miracles. It cannot inspire awe and make an impressive spectacle of itself. It cannot fight the princes of this world and frighten them into submission. A Protestantism which gets it into its head to become high and mighty in this world, believed and obeyed by the people, feared and respected by the powers around it, will only succeed in making itself ludicrous.

The present opportunity of Protestantism is its weakness, its helplessness among a helpless people, its fear among a frightened people, its chastened spirit among a chastened people. The Protestant churches have no authority, no power, no prestige, no keys to heaven or hell. They cannot pretend to possess and control God's truth, God's will, God's power. Their ways and means of inducing spirituality, compared with those of the Catholic Church, are childish and ineffective. Their minds are confused, their spirits are broken, their hands are tied. They do not know God's ultimate ends, they have no assurance of being repositories of God's grace and righteousness, they exercise no appreciable power in the world of economic and political conflicts.

A Protestantism true to its essence and intelligent about its task today will offer no ready-made and easy solution to the "problem of existence," no handbook of "the good life," no recipe for righteousness, no exercises for spiritual athletes. It will make no promises as to who shall sit on the right hand of the Lord when He comes "in His glory." It will be reserved in its idealism, humble about its highmindedness, and fearful about its spirituality. It will argue with diffidence, denounce with understanding, and exhort with patience. In all and above all, it will seek to voice the dumb cry of a humbled and despondent people for God, who alone can save them from sin and death.

Then it may be that Protestantism will rediscover the Gospel of Him who "came not to call the righteous, but the sinners." Then perhaps it will be able to preach the "Gospel of God," the good news of the forgiveness of sins and the resurrection of the dead. Then it may be that the hidden God will have mercy upon the people, and reveal His love in the repentance of the sinner. Then perhaps the Kingdom of God will come, *His* righteousness will dawn upon us, and we shall rejoice in His goodness towards us. Then perhaps we shall learn how to pray:

<table>
<tr><td>Our Father who art in heaven,</td><td>O God our Father who art not man,</td></tr>
<tr><td>Hallowed be Thy Name.</td><td>Make us to worship Thee, and not ourselves;</td></tr>
<tr><td>Thy Kingdom come,</td><td>Make us to obey Thee, and not ourselves;</td></tr>
<tr><td>Thy will be done on earth as it is in heaven.</td><td>Make us to serve Thee, and not ourselves.</td></tr>
</table>

Give us this day our daily bread.	Thou art the Giver of our daily bread—we do not earn it.
Forgive us our trespasses, as we forgive those who trespass against us.	Thou forgivest our sins, and persuadest us to love those who hate us.
Lead us not into temptation, but deliver us from evil.	Thou knowest that we are weak. Break Thou the power of evil, And deliver us from sin and death.
For Thine is the kingdom, and the power, and the glory, forever. Amen.	For Thou alone art God forever. Amen.

Chapter Two

ON THE PROTESTANT RELIGION

A. *ON THE LOVE OF GOD*

1. Religion for the Benefit of Man
2. Towards a Disinterested Love of God

B. *PROTESTANT INSIGHTS*

1. The Human Tragedy as Original Sin
2. A Protestant Discourse on the Problem of Evil
3. The Gospel of Jesus Christ
4. Election and Predestination

A. ON THE LOVE OF GOD

1. *Religion for the Benefit of Man*

THE REPUDIATION of anthropocentrism is a primary trait of the contemporary mind. Deep in the consciousness of the man of our time is the conviction that he is neither the center of his world nor the ultimate reason for it. He has been told repeatedly and on good authority that the realms of being are farflung beyond his imagining; that time has seen the birth and death of numberless creatures of a thousand kinds before he began to endure the moment of his existence; that the day of his world is only less brief than his own and will end in cold and prolonged lifelessness; that "science" does not countenance the eternization of human personality or of anything else. Our theologians have done their best to dissipate this impression created by modern knowledge. But the wiser of them have failed to convince even themselves. It is time to recognize that modern cosmogony has made anthropocentric religion, no matter how well disguised, very questionable indeed. In the long run, it may be suicidal for any religion of our time to dismiss the contemporary "scientific world view" with deficient argument, harangue, or derision.

"Values are more important than facts," "man is qualitatively superior to the whole cosmos," "man is the crown of evolution and the contemplator of the stars," "it is irrational to believe that the supremely valuable personality of man is not immortal," and like statements can hardly be expected to eradicate the feeling of insignificance produced by time and space, by the tortuous course of evolution and human history, and by nature's daily acts of violence against man and his values. A serious and genuine regard for the contemporary man's understanding of his place in nature and an honest revision of the anthropocentric religion of our day in the light of it have become necessary.

Our social experience leads us in the same direction. No one who is not afflicted with a serious case of intellectual myopia can rest secure in the delusion that he is of ultimate value in and to the community in which he exists. There is a profound incongruity between a man's significance to himself and his significance to others. His hunger and thirst, his fears and hopes, his pains and enjoyments, his "problem of existence," are his own concern. His will is repeatedly frustrated by the wills of others, his feelings and ideas are scorned by many who feel and think differently, his aims and ideals are constantly exposed to the opposition of his fellow men. No ultimate synthesis of his life with those of the people around him is possible. He must be prepared to suffer the alienation and neglect of his neighbors, and to endure loneliness in an overcrowded society. He must be prepared to receive good or evil, friendship or enmity, justice or injustice, help or hindrance. Futhermore no co-operation of his fellow men makes him secure against the larger obliviousness of society to his personal destiny in this world and in the next. A community is made up of many individuals; the nation, of many communities; mankind, of many nations. No man or community or nation is central in his or its social environment. In no case is the lesser the reason for the existence of the greater or the "last end" of it. The universe is not built around our planet, our planet does not exist for man alone, and "man" is not identical with any person in search of his private happiness. Such is the lesson the contemporary man has been learning slowly and painfully; and contemporary religion can ill afford to ignore it.

A radical critique of religion has become a necessity. We need to take it to heart that "religion" is man's first and last concern with his life and destiny. It is his ultimate bid for peace and happiness in a world of flux and contingency. It is his supreme effort towards eternalization and deification. Man who eats and drinks, fights and labors, in order to sustain the life in him; who shuns disease and the sword of the enemy; who enters into community existence and abides by its laws and mores, in order to enhance his power and security;

who "makes friends and influences people," in order that he may achieve mastery over his social environment; who sets out to control nature so as to avoid its rigors and to enslave its powers,—this same man makes idols and practises magic, worships and serves his gods, in order that he may have power over his destiny. Thus religion, with all the praise and honor it lavishes upon the deity, concerns man's own well-being, security, and happiness.

"Primitive religion" is unblushingly man-centered. It is directed towards the satisfaction of elementary human needs. Magic is practised towards definite ends: good crops and fertility in man and beast. Gods are feared and placated because they send the goods and evils in life. Taboos are set up and become effective because they define and stabilize the common life. Totems and well-supplied tombs create the delusion of continued life. Primitive religion is instrumental to the struggle for existence.

Reflective religion is always rather ashamed of itself and its lowly origins. It seeks to conceal its complicity with self-love by professing primary regard for its deities. It seeks to satisfy the ego of its god with elaborate rituals of hymn-singing, speech-making, and pretentious sacrifices of worldly goods; it praises, honors, glorifies, and serves him with great pomp and solemnity. Thus it pleases the people and their god at the same time. Thanks and gratitude are combined with cheerful expectation of the continued favor of the deity as essential elements in religion. Such religion achieves an ambiguous theocentricity which finds expression in "moral and ceremonial law." The whole life of man is brought *sub specie Dei;* God becomes over all and in all. Thanks are given, petitions are made, blessings invoked, sins are confessed and penance offered—all to God. From birth to death, in peace or in war, in sickness or in health, in poverty or in prosperity, in all things and at all times, God becomes a byword and a reality to be reckoned with. Religion flourishes, the priests prosper, the people enjoy themselves and are contented.

Thus magic and idolatry put on their ultimate disguise and human hypocrisy achieves the heights possible in religion alone. Now all tension between man and his world is dissipated in the noise and hubbub of man's celebration of his god. An indulgent deity accepts a few trinkets—song and sacrifice in return for his gifts of life and happiness. He becomes so inebriated with the adulation of his worshippers that he loves them one and all, forgives their sins in return for a prescribed and not too costly restitution, showers them with "the blessings of life," and assures them of life eternal when they die. Thus he achieves a benignity and deference to the wishes of his people which make him indeed worthy of their constant and most profound gratitude. Thus religion becomes at once theocentric and anthropocentric, and the problem of life is solved.

But alas, every so often, a strange misunderstanding emerges between the people and their deity, and disturbs the round of their happy fellowship together. Just when everything is going smoothly—God basking in the sun of human adulation and man rolling in the sea of "divine blessings"—God spoils it all with a visitation which terrifies and baffles his pious and complacent worshippers. Sin, disease, and death make the rounds of the people's homes, and the veil of sorrow is thrown over the face of the earth. Life ceases to be a celebration, and becomes a problem, a permanent and insoluble problem.

The priests and theologians get to work. By all means religion must be preserved. The people must be kept from doubt and despair which threaten their faith in their god. They must be kept cheerful, hopeful, active, zealous in religion. Otherwise social life will lose its sanctity and the social pattern will disintegrate. Hence no stone is left unturned towards the solution of the problems of sin and evil, suffering and death. "Suffering is punishment meted out by an angry deity. We have not been sufficiently zealous in our worship and obedience to his laws. . . . Evil is God's method of building character and preparing us for the reward of heaven. . . . Sin is the fruit of our free will; we are responsible for it, not God. God is good but not almighty. He has limited His power by creating the laws of nature and the free will of man. He is struggling with evil much as we are, and may well need our cooperation for its elimination, which will come sooner or later. . . . Since we can explain much of evil so excellently, we may well believe that the residue of it, which is negligible even though baffling, is according to the good but inscrutable counsel of God. . . . Death is only the doorway to the Beyond where we shall be free from all evil and enjoy permanent happiness. . . . In any case, we should continue in our piety as prescribed by our ancient and venerable religion."

The people acquiesce, but they are not convinced. Their faith weakens and their religion becomes lukewarm. Their good sense insists that there is something greatly wrong with a religion demanding that we overlook the many facts of evil and suffering which are incompatible with the principle that the end of the world is the happiness of man. The ways of nature and the desires of men do not coincide. Nature begets man; it gives him his food and drink, friends and progeny, and much joy. It also destroys crops, dries up wells, closes the womb, begets enemies, creates evil and sorrow, and finally cuts us off from life itself. Good and evil exist side by side from one end of life to the other, and turn human life into a problem which is solved by death alone. He is a fool who lets himself be talked out of the "problem of evil." The tragic sense of life is essential to the existence of the natural man endowed with the consciousness of time and limitation. It is rooted in the very self-consciousness of man, and can be set aside only through the prostitution of mind and conscience.

The ways of God stand in perennial opposition to the desires of men. Anthropocentric religion, even when disguised as consistently God-regarding religion, creates the problem of evil and is ruined by it. Its continued being is at the expense of reason and experience, as a half-justified product of "natural piety" which persists by means of the artificial stimulation of ceremonies and celebrations known as worship. When such expedients fail, it degenerates and becomes "natural religion." Its deities become the Unmoved Mover, the First Cause, the Great Designer, the Process of Integration, the Principle of Concretion, and the like, which hover around sophisticated minds and deceive the untutored into renewed piety. This also failing, religion degenerates further into moral idealism. God becomes the moral ideal and lives as a hope that the idealists will make him real. He remains good, but He ceases to exist. "Good riddance," says the noble-minded atheist.

The heart of anthropocentric religion is idolatrous. The essence of the folly of idolatry is the projection of human wish into the realm of the real. To call anything or anybody a god would be rather harmless were it not that we invest this our god with attributes derived from our private world of desire. Even when we become so sophisticated as not to take our visible idols seriously, we create invisible idols which again are fashioned after our wishes. We do not care much whether we see our gods with our eyes or with our minds. But we do care that they be bearers of our ideals, champions of our happiness, and ultimate vindicators of our ways. There is no essential difference between anointing a stone and sacrificing to a "higher" invisible *ba'al,* when the end of religion in both cases is the fertility of beast and vegetation. In either case man gets his crops and fills his belly. There is no essential difference between a war god and a god of justice and love. Both are worshipped towards the satisfaction of human want. One man has to fight and win; he worships a war god; the next man, indeed a better man, wants his goodness rewarded and his transgression overlooked; and *he* worships a god who is just and kind. Every man fashions his idols according to his "highest values." The hunter and the husbandman, the artist and craftsman, the philosopher, the warrior, and the business man, the mathematician and the reformer of public morals—all have ideals, all have idols. The better the ideals, the more conducive to health and happiness, the better the idols. But in any case, as is the heart, so is the idol or god. An idol may be just or unjust, loving or vengeful, dependable or not dependable. However, if he values his very being, no matter how rarefied, he had better serve his worshippers and reward them handsomely for their worship and service. Even an "ideal" is intolerable unless it is "practical." An idol which does not confer benefits seals his own doom and is discarded for what he is: a vanity. That is why idols, like peddlers of moonshine and rose-water, lead a precarious existence and one day wake up in the gutter.

Present-day Protestantism will do well to peruse deeply the Reformation polemics against idolatry. The particular idols which the reformers ridiculed and renounced no longer concern us very much. But the iconoclastic task of Protestantism is never at an end. Instead of images and relics, angels and saints, we have a god who has himself assumed all responsibility for catering to our desire for well-being, happiness, and security. We also have our minor gods of science and education, business and government, art and the sports, with their several priesthoods, passionate devotees, and elaborate rituals designed for the promotion of human happiness. Contemporary idealism, devoted to the desires of the human heart, and recognizing no instrument for their realization except man seeking "the good life," and bent upon exploiting "the human environment" for the increase of human happiness, is the ultimate in refined and hypocritical idolatry. This present-day religion, whether Christianity or idealism, is diametrically opposed to a Protestantism inspired by the Bible and the Reformers. And the duty of such Protestantism is to resist it without rest or recess.

2. *Towards a Disinterested Love of God*

Continued sin and death, symbols of the ultimate resistance of nature to human domination, expose the folly of anthropocentric religion, and become the foundations of a religion that is truly theocentric. The efforts of man to coax nature into radical subservience having failed, his chastened spirit learns, even if rarely, genuine respect for ends which are not his own. Repeated frustration of human desire produces a temper of heart and mind which leads to at least occasional recognition of nature's priority to man. When the rains pour down at the wrong time or a hot sun dries up the land and its fruits, on occasion, instead of finding "reasons," we tighten our belts and bow our heads in resignation. We refuse to "explain" the death of a much-needed parent or a healthy and promising youth. We have no apologies to offer for our sin and another's suffering. We cannot and therefore will not see any good accruing to mankind because of this war or that pestilence. In the midst of the dead ends and blind alleys of life, in our undramatic and non-celebrated anguish, in our gropings for the "meaning" of this or that misfortune, we stumble upon the unwelcome truth that the world is not explicable in terms of *our* desire for happiness and self-fulfilment. Thus it is that natural religion becomes untenable, and the way is opened for a supernatural or honestly theocentric religion.

Higher or theocentric religion emerges with man's awareness that he is not the center of the world. The first suspicion of the most primitive worshipper that his god has a will of his own is the seed of theocentric religion. The first recognition that there is a limit to divine subserviency and gullibility, to divine indulgence and pliability, to divine dependence upon the goodwill and worship of man, is the beginning of that religion which is based upon truth as well as human need. The first interpretation of human frustration as divine displeasure is the promise of a religion which can face facts as well as celebrate human desire. High religion is born when man hears God's "No!"

A religion is not high because its gods are few and big, or even when it has only one god. The perception of the world as a universe is no safeguard against idolatry; for, thanks to "original sin," man finds no difficulty in setting himself at the center of a universe. "God and my soul," he learns to say, "are the two foci of reality. . . . God is the circumference of the universe, I the center; God the origin, I the end; God the giver, I the receiver; God the father, I the child." No, monotheism is no guarantee against anthropocentrism, which is the essence of idolatry.

Post-exilic Judaism, with its one God and a law of God adequate for the removal of every guilt and the cure of all disease, was the high-water mark of magic in Hebrew religion. A monotheistic Christianity has made the doctrine of the Incarnation the basis for a legalistic and sacramentarian religion, and pretended that the Creator of heaven and earth resides in temples made by human hands and has placed Himself at the disposal of the priests and their followers. Protestantism is not appreciably superior to Catholicism in this matter. The latter constrain their Deity with their sacraments and works. They at least make a mystery of their idolatry. The way of the Protestants is simpler and easier. It seems that three hymns and a prayer are enough to satisfy their god, their *one* god, and to reduce him to a more or less dignified servitude.

The height of a religion is not to be measured even by the excellence of its morals. Increased insight into the conditions of public and private happiness can improve moral standards without effecting any radical alteration in the perspective of a religion. When a people attribute justice and kindness to their deity, they may do little more than to recognize that such qualities are conducive to human welfare. (Besides, it is far more comfortable to worship a "God of love" than one who is given to retributive justice.) The discovery that "war doesn't pay" may cause the transformation of a god of war to a god of peace. Social stability may require that the gods as well as men restrain their feelings and appetites, and have regard for the wants of others. Idols, which have little to say as to what characters they shall have, become objects of moralistic fancy and function as examples and proposed objects of human imitation. Even when possessed of highest moral attributes, they become instrumental to purposes which high-minded moralists entertain for the benefit of the people. They often become vague and changeable as a maiden's fancy, and not much more effective in the world of facts. Men pay them fulsome lip service and live their daily lives as though they had never heard of them. Thus idolatry inspired by "moral idealism" ceases to be even a genuine social force and becomes primarily an occasion for public hypocrisy. Gods whose primary function is to personify the moral ideals of men are idols and suffer their fate of change and decay. God, the Creator of the ends of the earth, speaks to man, saying: "My thoughts are not your thoughts, neither are your ways my ways. . . . For as the heavens are higher than earth, so my ways are higher than your ways, and my thoughts than your thoughts."

God, to whom high or theocentric religion turns, is the Other who will not yield His freedom and sovereignty to men. He will not fashion His world after the desires and purposes of the human heart. He will not adapt His government so as to suit it to our need and folly. He will not guarantee to provide for us; He will not give us signs and perform wonders according to our fancy and request. Instead, He will remind us, day in and day out, that His thoughts are not our thoughts, neither are our ways His ways. He will insist upon letting us suffer hunger and thirst, upon creating and sustaining life which often destroys our own, and upon letting evil men prosper. He will scandalize and torment us by sending rain when we wish sunshine, war when we want peace, poverty when we want riches, suffering when we desire happiness, and death when we yearn for life. He will confound us with *His* justice, upset us with *His* faithfulness, and wound us with *His* love. He will brand our love as sentimentalism, our justice as a bargain among thieves, and our goodness as ill-conceived love of ourselves. He will disagree with us and fail us, again and again. He will hide Himself, and will not be found of us.

A genuine theocentric religion is born of frustration. When we begin to heed the persistent rebuke life administers to our equally persistent self-love, when we begin to listen to the chastening refrain of the sun and the wind that the world is greater than man, when we begin to mix our murmurings and protests with decent interest in fortunes and interests other than our own, and try to measure good and evil with a yardstick other than our comfort and security, we begin to distinguish between the love of God and the love of ourselves. Theocentric religion is born in the midst of repeated frustration of desire, and flourishes with attention to the multiplicities of ends and destinies in our world. It comes into being in a lively struggle of intelligence and imagination against the irresistible and blind thrust of the life in us. It is the persistent conflict between flesh and spirit, between self-love and love of the other. When our natural attention to ourselves is disturbed with the perception of others as selves who resist our effort to make them instruments of our advantage, we are frustrated and hurt, but we also catch our first glimpse of truth. When man begins to temper his self-love with a recognition of ends other than his own and learns to become critical of his hope for happiness, when he turns from a reconciliation of ideal with fact and faces frustration with a certain dignity and tranquillity, when he even learns to oppose his struggle for existence with a steady attention to the decay and death all around him, he catches a glimpse of a religion which is fashioned by truth as well as desire.

The contemporary mind is deeply impressed with the admixture of good and evil in our world. The promiscuous way in which good and evil happen to the just and the unjust alike has led to the prevalent conviction that nature is indifferent to moral distinctions and operates without regard to moral standards. The readiness of nature to frustrate our purposes, to destroy our goods, to shatter our hopes, and to maim and kill us, has struck at the roots of "natural piety" and turned many men into quiet but confirmed atheists. Atheism is no less reasonable in the light of men's social experience. The willingness of men to destroy life and limb in order to secure power and security, the prosperity of the wicked who have cunning and power, the oppression of the weak and the exploitation of the helpless in our midst, and the thousand injustices which are woven into the fabric of society, make a moral interpretation of social life very questionable indeed. When one adds to these the agnosticism produced by "science" concerning the "existence of God," which has been received by many laymen with unquestioning faith, one realizes the extent to which anthropocentric religion has become unpalatable to the contemporary man.

Our priests and theologians had better stop kicking against the pricks. To violate the mind and conscience of our generation by constant preaching of man-centered religion, even when couched in the sublime terms of divine love and human excellence, is something of folly. A religion of high ideals and noble sentiment set up against our intuitions of plain truth cannot flourish in our midst. It is one thing to remind men of "truth, beauty, and goodness"; it is quite another to minimize their daily experiences of lies, ugliness, and wickedness. It is one thing to recognize the potentialities of man, quite another to ignore or apologize for the actualities of his behavior. There is a simple-minded prejudice in our midst to the effect that faith, hope, and love are induced by persistent mention of them in eloquent moralistic harangue. But, "brethren, let us love one another" is not enough. Contemporary religion must do justice to the quiet and confirmed hopelessness of the man of today. It must learn to speak the truth about man's place in nature, before it can inject true charity into our common life. It must join the people in "facing the realities of life," before it can offer a "religious interpretation of life" which shall be more than a series of pleasant but doubtful propositions about God and man. Instead of setting itself squarely against the pessimism, cynicism, agnosticism, and atheism of our time, it has to do justice to the facts which inspire these expressions of a chastened spirit in our day, and discover their roots in a praiseworthy willingness "to face the worst." Perhaps, when it thus partakes of the trial and tribulation of our common life, it will be able to speak the Word of God to a people who need Him but cannot find Him. Then it will be able to offer them a religion which will "ring true"; which will illumine their steps in this valley of the shadow of death.

Religion is a state of tension between persistent attention to one's selfhood and an equally persistent attention to the Other. Self-awareness and God-awareness are mutually necessary. The true self of man, the self revealed by sin-death, is the reason of our concern with God; it is the true subject of prayer to God; it is the real *man* who stands before God. Hence the door which opens into theocentric religion is an unflinching concern with the life and destiny of the self. There is no love of God in religion which does not involve the love of the soul or self. Thus religion is committed permanently to wrestle with the problems of sin, evil, and suffering. The religious man is bound to resist the temptation to achieve a disinterested or objective mind at the expense of concern with the human heart and its problems of life and integrity. He must learn to suffer deeply and unbearably because of man's inhumanity to man, because of the indifference of the fortunate and the malice of those who suffer wrong, because of the ubiquitous spectacle of unhealthy bodies, wasted minds, and disfigured souls. He must learn to share the horror and disgust which turn many an honest man into an atheist, and to cry aloud with him against this wasteland where virtue and happiness seldom dwell together. The problem of deliverance from sin, death, and hell cannot be set aside without destroying the very foundations of religious life.

In the midst of the struggle against sin and death, by a curious alchemy of heart and mind, the religious man undergoes a conversion which turns his attention to the not-self; now it dawns upon him that he is confronted with God's creatures which have their own life and destiny, and are prior to himself and his problems. His intense and persistent search for peace, confidence, and joy, his faithful preoccupation with the passion of his soul for integrity and reconciliation with life, his obstinate demand for meaning to his existence and reason for his restlessness, his refusal to shut his eyes to his ambiguous state as an animal who yet cannot live as a beast, his steady gaze at his insignificance in the midst of galaxies and eternities, his unsparing critique of the fears and follies within his own breast, together with the unbearable suffering they generate and inflame, lead him into the purifying fire of an anguish which transmutes his self-love into the love of God who is greater than the heavens and the earth and all the things therein. Not that his anguish is ever extinguished except when he neither thinks nor feels; it is rather that as he suffers, he is blessed; as he cries out, he is consoled; in his weakness, he is comforted; in his despair, he receives a peculiar and marvellous peace. At one and the same time, he is unspeakably miserable and equally blessed.

This conversion of man is the ultimate miracle of our existence, and has a peculiar relationship with self-consciousness and its products of self-love and self-seeking. It does not destroy the self and its works. From one end of life to the other, self-centeredness accompanies self-consciousness as a dog its master and produces our career of good and evil. At no time in their life do men cease to do evil and learn to do good. The ultimate possibility of man upon this earth is that of becoming a "repentant sinner." It is *as though* "self-love" were suspended, as though the sinner had become righteous, as though the evil we suffer had no unique significance for us, as though we were ready to die, as though we loved our neighbor as ourselves. We learn to love God, but not as we love ourselves. And yet this love marks our virtual deliverance from the sin and death in us, and is our only token of the unbroken life which is the permanent hope as well as problem of man.

The love of God manifests itself concretely as the miracle of compassion wherein we renounce our unique concern with the good and evil that come upon ourselves. The deeper sufferings of the heart which find their climax in the anguish caused by the fragmentary character of life, when not dissipated in riotous or listless living, seem to give us a strange power to appropriate the anguish and the deeper sufferings of the heart of another. It is as though the barrier of consciousness which condemns us each one to permanent aloneness is broken down and we confront each other in our essential humanity. . . . Consider what a miracle this is! My peculiar self is the product of the innumerable events which have gone into the making of my life. In these many years of intercourse with my environment, I have had a unique personal history, containing my hopes and fears, satisfactions and frustrations, loves and hatreds, shames and prides, courages and cowardices, thoughts and reveries, my million acts and imaginings. None of these things have happened to me as they have happened to any one else. In no one else have they ever produced a character identical with that which I call my own. They have covered the life in me with a thick and impenetrable covering and turned it into a private world of my own. Add to these conscious experiences of mine multitudes which have escaped my notice and yet are woven into my present self. Add also the much-debated influences which I owe to my peculiar heredity. Then consider how I have lived with all this in an intimacy which is essentially different from my familiarity with other bodies and their histories. And see now, if it is not an unbelievable thing that I should be able to break through all this accumulated selfhood of mine, and "feel with" another person. It is not surprising that such a feat should become possible only through the recovery of our common humanity which is our common anguish as we stand suspended between time and eternity, sin and righteousness, heaven and hell.

Compassion is the real ground of that willingness to "accept the universe" which must be distinguished from mere cultivated insensitivity. The contemporary man who does not permit himself to be drugged by the magic and mysticism of the several idolatries around him, is tempted to find peace and contentment in some species of impersonalism. He often tries to lose himself by cultivating an intense and steady passion for some impersonal aspect of life, and by giving himself up to it with maximum abandon. Science, the sports, literature and the arts, politics and business, are popular means of escape from the self and its private concern with time and transitoriness. They enable the people to "do something," to "pass the time," to "have fun." Thus they make men happy at the expense of self-consciousness, by reversion to subconsciousness, which is unnatural to *man,* and must necessarily issue in his degradation. Thus a man becomes a caricature of a human being; he loses his life without saving it. He loses himself in his work or play and becomes absorbed into the object of his interest. His life becomes a succession of satisfactions and failures, of pleasure and pain or love and hatred; while the self within him atrophies and ceases to have any genuine interest in reflection. He loses his sense of proportion and turns his life into folly. As a sportsman he plays to win and is devastated by loss of game or money. As a business man he knows more about making money than about using it. As a politician he becomes a hypocrite and a boor. As an intellectual he becomes a pedant, and as an artist he degenerates into a pompous juggler of word, color, or sound. Thus commerce, art, science, politics, sport, become sources of folly and complicate life rather than improve it. Man now becomes sentimental rather than sensitive, clever rather than wise, complacent rather than happy. Living in space rather than in time, he becomes a mere body and turns into a beast. (My apologies to the beast!) The neglected person within him takes his revenge by gradual suicide, and his heart of flesh is turned into stone. His selfhood degenerates into self-indulgence and a steady selfishness which can be tolerated only under thick coatings of hypocrisy and rationalization. Thus impersonalism destroys man's natural compassion for man and becomes a source of sin amongst us.

It is the peculiar business of religion to teach us how to "accept the universe" without losing our humanity. The perennial concern of religion with sin and death, time and eternity, and personal or moral relations, is the ultimate guarantee against the cheap and easy escape from the tragedy of manhood offered by the prophets of impersonality. Religion is the determination to hold on to our selfhood as the peculiar treasure of our humanity. Its history of magic and idolatry is sufficient evidence that on this point it knows no surrender or compromise. It has been and must remain anthropomorphic and anthropocentric in the sense that it must continue to wrestle with the problem and the problems of selfhood, with the "anguish of life" which is essential to the human self-consciousness. Whatever issues from religion, in theory or practice, must be rooted in the suffering of the self confronted with time and eternity.

On the other hand, and at the same time, a religion which stops short of "accepting the universe" has no alternative but idolatry. It flatters and deifies the self;

it seeks to satisfy self-love by destroying man's sense of proportion; it begets and breeds delusions of grandeur by setting man in the center of a world which has no center in it; it vomits lies about man's power over his past and his future by giving him the impression that he is a god; it demands assent to palpable falsehoods, obedience to "divine commandments" inspired by social need, participation in cults well calculated to produce a habitual sense of at-home-ness in the world and assurance of divine favor. It teaches the "truth," shows the "way," performs miracles, and promises rewards. Such religion confounds the intellect, deceives the conscience, and poisons the self into a prolonged sickness of dreaming dreams and seeing visions.

It is the function of religion to purify the whoredom of idolatry without resorting to the castration of impersonalism. It can do this only through an unwavering devotion to the problem of sin-death, while keeping a steady eye upon the impartiality of a sun which shines upon the good and evil and that of rain which falls upon the just and the unjust. It has to give heed to the soul's permanent restlessness in this world of partial fulfilments and ultimate frustrations, while it turns our attention to ends and purposes which are independent of our weal or woe. It must cultivate a temper which makes a man at once introvert and extrovert, passionate and dispassionate, personal and impersonal, self-centered and another-centered. It must set itself squarely against either side of these alternatives, and maintain a strong tension between them.

Our generation has a passion for "scientific objectivity." The enlightened among us love and cling to the notion that if we could only apply the "method of science" to human relations, we could solve most of the standing problems of society. One hears a great deal of appeal to disinterestedness, impartial observation, rationality, objectivity, and the like principles which are expected to make us imitators of the scientist in his laboratory and sharers of his triumphs of knowledge and power over the non-human environment. "Let us be scientific, and find out the true causes and effects of the events around us; and we shall know what to do with them! After all, human relations are merely more complicated versions of physico-chemical relations. Let us keep at it, and we shall soon gain mastery over social evil as we have over a great deal of natural evil."

This is a very hopeful theory; and were it true, the problem of ethics would be immeasurably simpler. But alas, there is one important flaw in it: it is based upon the assumption that the human self is merely a very complicated thing. Your "scientific" student of man is determined to pay minimum attention to the self's concern with time and eternity and to the problem of sin-death which issues from it. He will have nothing to do with the "anguish of life": with sin as the sickness of life and with death as the frustration of life. He studies assiduously and in detail the struggle for existence as manifested in a thousand deeds of good and evil, but he ignores man's conscious or unconscious anticipation of the ultimate outcome of this struggle as irrelevant to the conduct of life! Hence the "secret of life" escapes his knowledge, and with it also the secret of goodness and mercy in our midst. Any knowledge of social relations, no matter how systematic and inclusive, which tends to ignore the tragedy of man as a thinking animal, remains a poor instrument towards the mitigation of man's inhumanity to man.

Objectivity in religion stands in a state of permanent tension with thoroughgoing subjectivity. The religiously objective mind is fashioned in the fire of the soul's conflict with sin and death. This conflict reveals a world of men and things which can no longer be designated as nature. Nature is the world as it appears to the man who evades the anguish of the self within him. Hence it is "impersonal" and irrelevant to the problem of sin and death. The world as it appears to the self is bound up intimately with the problem of the self. It is the world in which we sin and we die. It is the world of sin and death. This is the reason for the severe judgments on the world which fill the literature of the Christian religion. The world as seen by the soul in anguish is a wasteland, a land of whoredoms, a valley of the shadow of death. *This* is the world which the religious man is called upon to contemplate objectively. See how easily he sinks back into the quagmire of self-love and loses himself in the Sodom and Gomorrah of preoccupation with things! The human soul must pass through the fires of purgatory nearest to hell, before it can catch a glimpse of the "disinterested love of God."

Objectivity in religion becomes a possibility when our neighbor is discerned through the veil of sin and death cast upon all things upon this earth. In the same travail of the soul, we discover ourselves and the world as a community of selves, and thus achieve a virtual triumph over the sin in us. We discover our neighbors, and thus confront the possibility of loving them as ourselves. We are now men among men, creatures among creatures, those who sin and die among those who sin and die. Such are the roots and first fruits of objectivity in religion.

It is now as though the spell is broken. A curious catharsis is set to work in the human soul. When we cease to suffer alone, our very suffering becomes blessed. As the self meets other selves, its anguish is transfigured into a wisdom and understanding peculiar to religion. Without ceasing to be anguish, it loses its former sting and bitterness. Its pain is no longer its own; its sorrow is no longer a private mystery; its hopes and fears are no longer passions of a solitary self. Without losing its selfhood, it ceases to be in bondage to its own irritations and despairs. Thus it loses itself, and finds itself anew.

It is the self which was dead, and is alive again; a miracle of creation, a self capable of being objective, of suffering with others.

A summary solution of the problem of evil as given by naturalism (Nature is indifferent to good and evil) is not possible for the religious mind. The latter sees the world as a mixture of good and evil having its origins in the nature of things. Its basic intuition that being is opposed to non-being as good is opposed to evil, forbids any circumvention of the interpretation of life in terms of good and evil. It can have no traffic with the conception of a "neutral universe," because its world is a mixture of lights and shadows surrounded by the total darkness of non-being. Endowed with the tragic sense of life, the religious man may and does despair; but he cannot set aside the problem of evil because he cannot set aside his anguish; and he cannot set aside his anguish because it is his essence and very manhood.

Religious objectivity does not escape the problem of evil; it transforms it from a private to a public affair. The mind, having entered into a world of selves, begins to see sin and suffering as ubiquitous, and the problem they present it as objective to itself. Thus the problem of evil becomes wide as the world; the anguish it accompanies becomes almost insufferably intense, and the quest for a solution of it doubly impossible to abandon. However, it is also radically altered. The problem of evil which in self-centered religion is indistinguishable from the problem of suffering, now becomes prior to and far more urgent than the latter. The heart-mind, having turned from itself to the other selves, proceeds to concern itself with the source of evil. It presents itself with the terrible possibility that the Determiner of Destiny is evil. For a moment it forgets its own despair and contemplates God as the Great Enemy. Strangely enough, now it seems to care more about justifying God than about mitigating its own suffering. The suffering of the whole world thus becomes a lesser problem than the problem of God, of the goodness of God. By a miracle of conversion, hardly believing its own ears, the agonizing soul mutters: "Let me perish. Yes, let the whole world perish. But let it not be true that God is evil." Thus it begins to love God with a new love, with a truly holy and disinterested love. Thus the anguish of life, with its problems of suffering and evil, becomes the foundation of a truly theocentric religion.

B. PROTESTANT INSIGHTS

1. *The Human Tragedy as Original Sin*

The failure of contemporary Protestantism to do justice to the tragedy in human life robs it of the power and dignity of truth and disqualifies it as a religion for the contemporary man. A religion consisting of belief in "God, freedom, and immortality" makes scant provision for a serious view of the veil of sorrow covering the race of mankind. Men who imagine their God as One whose chief concern is their happiness, who trust in their "moral ability" to be good and to do good, who expect their "abundant life" here to issue in a life of perfect happiness after death, become well-nigh incapable of a living sense of tragedy. Their cultivated complacency removes the sting of the sin within them and makes their mortality a meaningless fact. They live as though they were without sin, as though they were immortal. Their life is turned into a lie and smothers the anguish of the soul within them. Their faith is turned into an inexpensive opiate and becomes an object of laughter and derision to the unbelievers.

Historic Christianity preserved its faith and hope

from such folly through an honest and persistent attention to the misery of mankind upon this earth. Its doctrine of Original Sin was a profound tribute to the sin and suffering of life confronted with death: "The whole race of mankind, beginning with the first man, have lived and continue to live under a curse which condemns them to sin and to die." All the sons of Adam, the multitudes who have lived and died upon this earth, the black and the white, the rich and the poor, the free and the slave, the good and the evil—each man being a private world of love and hatred, pleasure and pain, hope and despair—all "flesh and blood," all *people*, all *souls*, come into this world equipped for sin, suffering, and death. Yea, they all sin, they all suffer, and they all die. What a spectacle of human misery is revealed by this vision of universal sin and death! What sobering and wholesome truth lay embedded in this doctrine of the Christian Church! It is a tell-tale evidence of the superficiality and silliness of contemporary Protestantism that it has relegated this historic teaching to the limbo of benighted falsehoods. Bewildered by the myth of the fall of Adam, scandalized by the fact that one man's sin neither remains nor dies with him, our tender-minded theologians turned away from the obvious and palpable fact of public, inherited, and communicated sin and suffering. These sunny-minded lovers of God and friends of humanity, with one breezy sweep of delicate sentiment, eliminated the very foundation of compassion in our vision of our common sin and death.

The common tragedy of mankind reveals the radical character of sin and evil in our world. It is written in the constitution of man and his world that he should sin and die. His very flesh (his body and soul) condemns him to cruelty. He inherits the lust for life, and his world presents him with the necessity of death. Life moving towards death becomes a living death and a dying life. As living death it becomes sin and cruelty, as dying life it becomes sorrow and suffering. Life suffers as it sins and sins as it suffers. In this vicious circle appears inhumanity. A necessity is laid upon man to seek power, to exploit, to oppress, and to enslave. The fear, restlessness and despair within his breast issue in sin as sparks fly upwards. The whole world is filled with thistles and thorns, and groans with pain.

The world in which we live as neighbors to each other is a wasteland. We enter into it as we perceive the evil and not the good in it. "The good things of life" are evanescent and ambiguous. They are shadowy goods we embrace in our persistent effort to escape the devastating intuition that life, the condition of all good for us, is predestined for frustration. They separate us from each other and place us in private worlds of pleasure and complacency. When we rejoice we rejoice alone, unless our rejoicings adumbrate our common sorrow. There is no true and profound perception of our common life except in confrontation with our common sin and death. Our true brotherhood consists in our common destiny of frustration in body and soul, rather than in our common origin through the accident of birth into this world. Our lives as individuals, beginning with our birth, make us strangers and enemies. In our sin anticipating our death, we became fellow men, sons of Adam, members of the race of mankind. In our original sin we are truly and unavoidably brothers: brothers to the black and to the white, to the rich and to the poor, to the wise and to the foolish, to the oppressor and to the oppressed, to the living and to the dead.

Therefore, we are not brothers in Christ unless we are brothers in Adam; and we are not brothers in Adam except as we partake of Original Sin. Our faith and our hope bind us together because of our common need for deliverance from sin and death, and light the flickering candle of love within us. The perception of our common misery in our inherited and communicated disease of sin and in frustrating death, co-operating with our faith and hope in Christ Jesus, is the true origin of a lively struggle against self-centeredness and the censoriousness and cruelty which accompany it. It initiates that understanding or love which is the first and last need of our fellow sufferers. It weakens our zeal to judge and to condemn. It puts to shame the ubiquitous desire for retaliation and revenge which is veiled as justice and fills the world with injustice and suffering. Thus, the love of God, shed abroad in our hearts by the Spirit proceeding from the Father of our faith and from the Son who died and rose from the dead unto our hope, struggles against the sin within us, and brings us to our knees in a contrition which is at all times the surest evidence of the compassions kindled within us.

The common *excuse* for present-day aversion to the conception of Original Sin is that the Biblical story of the Fall of Adam has been exposed as a myth. The chief *reason* for it is the moralism in our religion which exalts responsibility at the expense of charity. Moralism resists the fact of our unfailing and almost certainly inevitable sinfulness because it recoils before the notion that we are necessarily sinners. "If we are condemned to sin by our present nature, then how can we be held responsible for our sins? For if we have no free will, then we are not responsible. And if we are not responsible, then our 'moral agency' is unreal and the foundations of morality are destroyed. But this must not be. Hence we must combat the subversive notion of Original Sin and cling to our belief in the freedom of the will. We must hold men accountable for their misdeeds. We must leave them without excuse. We must bring them to judgment before God, or conscience, or, if necessary, before our courts of law. Hence, we repudiate solemnly and immovably the antiquated and immoral notion that men are in bondage to sin inherited as 'flesh' and perpetuated necessarily in the process of life." Thus, moralism makes the indirect coercions of society the true foundations of public morality and glorifies hidden fear as the highest inducement to right living. The common desire for safety in any given group of people, which underlies much of the exercise of conscience, puts on a respectable mask, and passes for "morality." Our theorists flatter it as "the voice of God." They praise its calculated uprightness and try to forget its failure to be an effective antidote to the inhumanities generated by the common struggle for existence. Thus "moral agents" continue to sin, and soothe their consciences with frequent ablutions of noble sentiment. Good intentions and occasional regrets are woven into a thick covering and made to conceal our actual injustice, callousness, and vengefulness. And the devil continues to rule the world as the power behind the double throne of our benevolence and idealism. Especially in this our day when even believers no longer care to think of God as engaged in distributive justice, when the connection between the dictates of conscience and the consequences of obedience or disobedience to it have become uncertain, and when "practical sense" plays havoc with the moral, responsibility has become a precarious foundation for righteousness. Whatever "free will" is (and this is no place for reviving the now threadbare controversy on the subject), its contribution to love among men is indeed doubtful and ambiguous.

The repudiation of the doctrine of Original Sin in favor of the doctrine of "free will" has minimized men's perception of the tragedy of life which is immeasurably superior to the sense of responsibility as a foundation for charity among men. Our "moral sense" sets us apart from other individuals and creates only a superficial harmony between their wills and ours. Our sense of responsibility operates mainly through fear of social opposition and defeat in the hands of those who disapprove of our ways. Thus, the enmity between men as those in a struggle for existence suffers no profound modification through the ordinary operations of conscience. Such modification becomes possible only through the perception of the one peculiarity of *human* life: anguish before death and the sin which accompanies it. Charity among men is conditioned by the tragic sense of life embedded in the doctrine of Original Sin rather than by "faith in man" embedded in the modern versions of the doctrine of free will. We are one, "sons of Adam," "members of the race of mankind," in our sin and death, far more consistently and truly than in our highmindedness and in our power over the sin in us generated by the struggle for existence, and intensified as well as concealed by *our* reason and conscience.

It is disastrous to forget that Christianity and moralism were neither born together nor will die together.

Historic Christianity, including the Reformation theology, has never denied that freedom of will whereby men are responsible for their sins. But it has repeatedly shied away from the moralistic heresy. It has recognized that man is in bondage to the sin within him and cannot deliver himself by means of a spontaneous somersault of the will. It has known and taught that the miracle of man's liberation from sin is rather connected with his perception of his bondage. It has upheld the doctrine of the weakness of the "flesh" and sought to awaken men to the necessity of the Gospel of Divine grace in Jesus Christ: the Gospel which present-day moralism or Pelagianism has made superfluous and unattractive. Thus it has constrained men to turn to *God,* in prayer and contrition, and exposed them to the power of God which alone can deliver them from sin and death.

Let us be clear on this point. A doctrine of "the freedom of the will" which makes men's sense of obligation the original basis of the good life transforms Christianity into a religion of law and nullifies the historic doctrine of grace. It is a revival of that legalism which the Church has always resisted because Christianity is the faith that *God* in Christ Jesus forgives sins and justifies the sinner. The Christian life is a work of God, a wonderful and mighty work of God, wherein our wills become subject to God rather than to Satan, and we *will* that God be obeyed freely and truly. It is the miracle of faith whereby we hope for our justification and resurrection. This faith operates through the Cross of Christ which reveals the fullness of the evil of sin and makes repentance a terrible necessity. Indeed, the persuasion of God which leads us to repentance is received voluntarily, with fear and joy. But it is the love of God, and not the "freedom of the power of the faculty of will," that the repentant sinner recognizes as the true cause of his justification. The Christian acknowledges his bondage to sin, and rejoices in the power of God who delivers him from it. The moralist rejoices in the power of his will, and trusts that it will make him virtuous. . . . There is no way of proving to the moralist that he is justified by faith and not by his works. There is no way of proving to him that the forgiveness of God is the true foundation of the good life. There is no way of proving to him that the poor in spirit alone enter into the Kingdom of heaven. In short, God alone can turn a moralist into a Christian, and give him the freedom of a son of God. . . . There can be little doubt that a rejection of the doctrine of Original Sin in favor of the doctrine of "free will" is tell-tale but telling evidence of a religion which is pagan rather than Protestant.

For the contemporary mind, with its "scientific outlook," its deep perception of the sovereignty of the "flesh," its persistent suspicion of selfishness lurking underneath our altruism, and its realistic emphasis upon the follies and cruelties of mankind, a religion based upon "faith in man" and moral responsibility must remain unpalatable. Thank God, there has come to be a limit to our gullibility and sentimentalism. We can no longer take seriously and expect to live by the perorations of pulpit orators concerning our unlimited potentialities. Our repeated sins and follies make us doubtful concerning the power of our free will which we are asked to magnify in the interests of Christian morality. We can no longer be persuaded by fulsome talk on what we *can* do, at the expense of proper attention to what we do daily and persistently. We would live in the misery which truth may impose upon us, rather than enjoy happiness and hope through artificial optimism. We enjoy spirited sermons on high ideals and profess admiration for "Jesus' way of life"; nevertheless we continue to obey the necessities of an existence circumscribed by conflict and ultimate frustration. Hence it were wise for our religious leaders to accept sincerely and wholeheartedly the truth and fact in contemporary "cynicism"; yea, to awaken the hearts and minds of the men of our day to their bondage to sin and death, and thus to give them a lively sense of the anguish within them which they seek to silence and ignore.

Historic Protestantism and contemporary naturalism which is not purely academic agree in their recognition of the power of the "flesh" and of the ambiguity of man's responsibility for his sin and death. In this they are set squarely against the optimistic but myopic religion of our day. Both have discovered that sinfulness is prior to any act of sin and is rooted in a "nature" which men receive rather than create. Nature without and nature within, reinforced by the nature of human society, make the "moral freedom" of the individual precarious indeed. On the other hand, the propagation of sin through inheritance and infection, as well as the reality of a common nature exposed and even condemned to sinfulness, are truths which no moralism can destroy, no religion can afford to ignore or pass over lightly. Protestantism will fail to commend itself to the serious consideration of the contemporary man unless it learns to share his despair in the midst of recurrent and overpowering sin and thus to mix its futile exhortations with revealing truth concerning the origins and consequences of sin. The mythology of the doctrine of Original Sin may sound strange to the ears of the modern man. But the truth it sets out to impress upon us, the tragic covering of sin and death upon the face of God's "intelligent creation," is profoundly congenial to his mind and must be included in the preaching of the Word of God to him. This doctrine is the Protestant's chief claim to genuine reverence for fact, the first bond between him and the chastened spirits of our time, the only constraining evidence that the Gospel of Jesus Christ is indeed the Word of God for this generation.

A Protestantism which can no longer understand it is neither Protestant nor contemporary. It is simply silly. Our preachers owe it to the truth, to the contemporary man, and to the faith they preach, to rediscover the doctrine of Original Sin and to replace it where it belongs in the Christian Gospel.

Protestantism accentuates this doctrine and preserves it against dilution with the doctrine of "total depravity." The Protestant reformers repudiated the semi-Pelagianism of the Catholic Church, and insisted that the whole of man, his reason as well as his will, were corrupted with the Fall: that there is no good thing left in him. Both Luther and Calvin used strong language with regard to human depravity: language which has become unpalatable to our age. So be it. It is once again an evidence of the foolishness of contemporary Protestantism that it cannot see the point of this doctrine: the basic anti-Catholic conviction that man has no power over sin and death. The doctrine of "total depravity" is a symbol of the Protestant's radical repudiation of the Catholic conception of meritorious deeds which accompanies the subtle magic in Catholic religion. A Protestantism which denies this doctrine is without an essential and consistent defense against Catholicism. It lines itself up with the kind of religion which sets itself to create the illusion that man has the power and means for destroying his past and altering his ultimate destiny. It stands in opposition to the contemporary insight that *all* man's acts and deeds are powerless to deify him. "Total depravity" and "justification by faith" are expressions of the same conviction that man's one hope against perdition is God.

2. *A Protestant Discourse on the Problem of Evil*

Strangely enough, the doctrine of Original Sin was meant to explain the origin of sin as well as to establish man's need for God. The Christian theologians sought to hold man responsible for his sin while they recognized its roots in the constitution of human life in this world. The facts were plain: Man sins because he is man, and he sins in the exercise of his reason and will, consciously and willingly. Thus the roots of sin are in man himself or in his will. And yet the will is received as well as exercised. Men *will* to sin because they are men, because they lust for life, and confront death. Their manhood is a given thing, and the Giver of it must be the ultimate cause of sin. When this fact was pressed upon the theologians with a question such as: Why did a good God create men bent upon rebellion and disobedience? they hesitated, objected, and even threatened the inquirer with hell-fire. But they were unable to escape the conclusion that God the Creator of heaven and earth "willed" and "decreed" evil as well as good. "I form the light, and create darkness; I make peace, and create evil; I am Jehovah, that doeth all these things."

God has never been successfully cleared of His share in the making of the world's evils, except at the expense of His sovereignty, or creatorship, or even His existence! The theory of a limited God, entertained in some quarters, is a subterfuge. Bifurcating the world, attributing the good in it to God and the evil in it to forces independent of Him, is possible only in a mind independent of its world. Where, pray, in the real world, is the line to be drawn? What is the work of God, and what is not the work of God? Are winds and storms and insects and beasts of prey works of one who is other than He who made the sun, the good earth, the shady trees and the beasts of burden? Or, what in man is of God and what not of Him? Which instincts, passions, or desires are of God, and which not of Him? What deeds of men reveal the hand of God, and which of them do not? Is the exercise of the will independent of God? Where, pray, shall we draw the line? Who will draw the line for us? Nobody can. It is the permanent lot of the religious mind to live in such a world, and to cry out its faith in the goodness of God.

The more common solutions of the problem based upon the notion of free will are unsavory for Protestants who are mindful of the essentials of their religion. The contemporary passion for free will undermines the foundations of the Protestant case against magic and idolatry. Luther renounced the notion of free will because he saw it as an essential part of a religion of works and merits. He trusted the power of God rather than his own freedom to overcome sin and death. Hence similarly, for the most astute of Protestant thinkers on this subject, Jonathan Edwards, moral agency consisted in voluntary behavior, which is a *fact*, and not in the possession of a free faculty of will, which would make moral behavior merely indeterminate and therefore mechanical rather than moral. Man wills and acts as he does because he is man, as the sun gives light and heat because it is the sun; he wills and acts according to his nature which he inherits from Adam, and in conformity to the "greatest apparent good." Besides, to ascribe the sin and evil in the world to an elusive and ambiguous faculty in man, while we readily ascribe all good to God, violates our perception of the roots of both good and evil in the nature of things, and undermines the foundations of the Protestant case against magic and idolatry. A tough-minded Protestantism with honest reverence for facts is committed to the propositions that man is made so that he can and does sin, and that in some sense the Creator decrees "evil" as well as "good."

Of course, the subject of "divine decrees" confronts us with great and perhaps insuperable difficulties. The problem of God's actual relationship to His creation involves the problems of the eternal and the temporal, the necessary and the contingent, the primary and the secondary, the one and the many, etc., which are perennial riddles of philosophy, and suggest that the world must forever remain a mystery to us. The explanation of the permanence of controversy on these subjects must be sought in the religious interests of those who have been engaged in them as well as in their philosophical insight. Modern Protestants, whose religion is inspired by their faith in man and nature, have little difficulty with the conception of a limited God. Reformation Protestantism, which was inspired by the problem of deliverance from sin and death, held tenaciously to its faith in the sovereignty of God and believed passionately in His power over man and nature. It was indeed embarrassed by the logic of its faith, and qualified it by recognizing moral agency and natural causation. Nevertheless, it held fast to its faith in a sovereign Creator and Redeemer, and expressed it almost defiantly in the formula that God decrees evil as well as good.

The willingness of historic Protestantism to entertain this terrible conclusion is its witness to a tough-mindedness which is absent from contemporary Protestant religion. Not even the severest critics of religion could have accused the former of wishful thinking. The religion of men like Calvin and Edwards involved an unflinching attention to fact and an unswerving willingness to entertain ideas which scandalized self-love, but corresponded to the truth as they saw it. A man like

Edwards had too much respect for his religion to believe that it required dishonesty and wishful thinking. If the Creator has made man and the world so that sin and death are both possible and real, then He has done it. When man learns reverence for fact, the Creator Himself takes care of His honor and good name. Reverence for truth is the foundation of faith and piety in religion which has learned to renounce magic and idolatry.

The first principles of tough-minded religion, needed badly in our day, received striking formulation from Jonathan Edwards, perhaps the first and greatest of those who sought to incorporate the spirit of modern science and empiricism into Christian theology. "We may justly infer what God intends, by what He actually does; because he does nothing inadvertently, or without design." "In God there are no distinctions to be admitted of faculty, habit, and act, between will, inclination, and love. But that it is all one simple act." "On the one hand, the decrees of God are no other than His eternal doing what is done, acted or executed by him in time. On the other hand, God's acts themselves, in executing, can be conceived of no otherwise, than as decrees for a present effect. They are acts of God's will. God brings things to pass only by acts of His will. He speaks, and it is done." "He wills to permit sin, it is evident, because He *does* permit it. . . . He wills what is contrary to excellency in some particulars. for the sake of a more general excellency and order."

Such genuine reverence for fact would have a cathartic and invigorating effect upon contemporary Protestantism. It would provide the foundations for a discipline in religious thinking which is badly needed in our time. It would balance the element of wishful thinking in religion with a fruitful attention to the realities of life. It would clear the turgid waters of religious thought by removing from it a great many fanciful opinions about man, nature, and God, which have to be entertained "by faith," at the expense of fact and rigorous thought. "Human personality is of infinite value." Where and how did any one find this out? Look at any man you please, and tell me how you deduce that he is infinitely valuable. "Nature is instrumental to the formation of highest human character." The whole universe travailing, age upon age, to the end that I acquire a "high character!" Now, where did any one find this out? "God does not will the unhappiness of a single man." How, in the name of truth, do you know? Was it not told you by your "moral sense," which is never above contamination by self-love? How can you deduce such a thing from observation? If all the unhappiness in the world is contrary to the will of your God, then do you seriously believe that you can find His works anywhere except in the complacency of the callous? If all the evil in the world is independent of Him, can you find a creature who declares His glory and shows His handiwork—without ambiguity? Once you have set out to divide the world into a set of goods and a set of evils, what will deliver you from your folly and confusion except that you should learn to glorify God because of "evil" as well as because of "good," that you should learn to understand rather than judge, that you should allow the truth to judge you rather than you the truth, that you should learn to dissociate God's purposes from your preferences?

It is essential that the religious man struggling with this problem of evil equip himself with a mind capable of being critical of desire. Self-love needs to be constantly and profoundly chastened by fact. The ubiquitous facts of frustration require more than explaining away. They necessitate a religion which will teach men their actual relationship to the world in which they exist; which can take seriously and communicate effectively the fact that no man, no race of men, no generation of men, is "the last end for which God created the world." It is a primary duty of true religion to expose our folly when we imagine that man is the center of the creation, the ultimate reason for the existence of the sun and the stars, of rain and winds, of the trees in the jungles and the flowers on the hillsides, of the beasts of the fields and the fowls of the air. To what nation, or race, or people, or class, or any other division of mankind, has the Lord said: "You are My chosen. I have set you aside to rule and to have dominion, to exploit and to enjoy forever"? And what person in what group or division of this race of inflated egos exhibits anything but most sinful folly when he acts as though his group or division exists for his good and happiness? Will not the group continue to be after he is gone, as the human race will go on after his group is dispersed and lost, as the world will exist after our race is dead, as God will still be God after our world is destroyed? The whole "constitution of the world" is clear indication that no creature is God's last end in creating the world; that the manifestation of Divine glory through all creatures and destinies is the true and final end of the existence of all things.

What a caricature of true greatness it is when man begins to strut around, and to think haughty thoughts; when he occupies the center of the stage, and calls upon God to think his thoughts and to walk in his ways; when he scorns the "lower creation," plucks and plants, builds and destroys, without reverence and as he pleases. "All things are for me," says the fool, "the soil, the air, the waters, the plants, the beasts—all are mine and for me. God made all things for me. God Himself is for me. He had better seek my good. He had better keep me from evil, as I see evil. He had better serve me, or, by my exalted sense of justice, I will cease to worship Him. If He dares to ruin my crops or kill my cow, I shall say to Him: 'You are not God. You are not good. You do not even deserve to exist. You shall not exist, I shall call You nature or fate, and I shall not love You, nor praise You, nor believe in You.' "

The seeds of the true greatness of man are sown when he becomes aware of a world of many ends independent of the self and his private career. When creatures not ourselves are recognized, even dimly, as entities whose origins and histories are their own and not ours, as beings having their private ends and purposes, their own feelings and reactions, creatures which rejoice in their own good and sorrow over their own evil, which are born, and grow, and die for themselves–*human* rationality comes to its own and we begin to discern the outlines of the image of God in the human soul. But alas, the "cares of this world" are soon upon us. When our purposes are repeatedly frustrated by the self-love of others, when man and nature seem to join hands in working towards our unhappiness, we set ourselves to "look out for ourselves" and to harm others before they harm us. We taste the bitterness of this dying life in expectations of man's and nature's inclemencies at the most unexpected times, and the fear in us transforms our self-love into deep-rooted and permanent selfishness. This sin in us establishes the delusion that our self, its career and destiny, are central to the universe and alone of ultimate importance.

Thus every man comes to have two principles within him: the spirit and the flesh, which strive against each other, even to the end of our days. The flesh, a poisoned love of life, is much the stronger, and by nature dominates the human soul. The spirit is whipped into submission and persists as superfluous idealism and imaginary sanctity. The occasional triumphs of the spirit over the flesh are won only by the fiercest and most reckless battling, and are never achieved without terrible wounds and deep agony. The life of the spirit is at all times one of suffering joy, of tense and watchful peace. It is lived in the purgatory of trial and temptation, invigorated by frustration and refreshed by a mysterious blessedness in the midst of the threats and promises of the flesh.

The priceless reward of this struggle is a "Copernican revolution" wrought in the human heart-mind. In the midst of the wear and tear of our sin-infested existence, we begin to catch glimpses of a "supernatural light" which gives us a new vision of our world. The things in heaven and upon the earth begin to take their proper places in "universal being," and their true proportions emerge gradually with the lifting of the fog of our man-centered perspective. Instead of treading a tortuous and dreary path around *us*, they begin to circle blithely around a center which is here, there, and everywhere. We gaze in amazement at the intricate patterns they weave around each other, at the ease of their movements and at the innocence of their ways. We see the sun shining upon the good and the evil, the moon smiling at lovers and haters alike, the stars, so tiny and so unassuming, pouring peace and serenity upon the whole earth. Night and day, cold and heat, seedtime and harvest-time, the four seasons and the many years, succeed one another with steady indulgence and generosity, laden with wisdom and love. The trees flourish and give fruit; they grow old and die. The flowers fill the world with scent and beauty; they grow weak and wither away. Eggs become animals and produce eggs. There are eating and drinking, mating, running and fighting, howling, chirping, and neighing. There are victory and defeat, pain and pleasure, pity and cruelty, many lives and many deaths. Then there are men, women, and children, millions of them; rich and poor, high and low, wise and foolish, well and unwell, black, yellow, and white. These also live and die. They *all* are themselves and no one else. They fill the world to overflowing. We are among them, with them, and for or against them. We all live in the same world of which the Center is neither they nor we ourselves.

To live in a world with many centers, to live knowing that nobody and nothing is the center of the world, is what Edwards called "the love of Being in general." It is a disposition of heart-mind which enables one to love with the understanding and to understand with love. It is that compassion which depends as much upon light as upon warmth, and surrounds itself with justice as well as kindness. It is that disinterestedness which is begotten of the mind's attending to the others, of the will to recognize the private ends and destinies of the creatures around us and to become instruments of their realization. It is the "love of being simply considered," the love of each and any being as a real and unique entity.

God's love is revealed through being in general. The love of the same God is made manifest in nature and in man. God loves all His creation. He creates what He loves, and loves what He creates. All beings manifest the love of God by being what they are. God loves the beasts as beasts, and men as men. They all declare His glory—His wisdom, power and goodness—and are witness to God's activity whereby all things are what they are. They all are, to use Edwards' terminology," "refulgences of His internal glory," "communications *ad extra*" of that eternal Being who is greater than all created being.

However, the ant does not have the same "being" as a horse, and the horse does not possess the nature peculiar to "intelligent being." Christianity and man-equals-ape naturalism are not compatible with each other. God feeds the fowls of the air and clothes the lilies of the field. "How much more you, O ye little of faith!" Man is created "in the image of God"; he is made little lower than the angels. The fact is that he walks on two legs, uses speech and tools, reasons and writes, remembers and repents, agonizes about sin and death. Man is not created a beast; he can only degenerate into one. He must glorify God with his understanding love and obedient service, not as the birds which chirp God's praises, and not as the winds which howl it.

Today we are torn between two follies. Our theologians, with not too great subtlety, tell us we are as gods, "created creators!" Our "scientific naturalists," with not too great humility, tell us we are as beasts. So, we act like beasts, and feel like gods. It is difficult to conceive a situation more conducive to human degeneration. Christianity demanded that we obey God, and confess our sins. It taught us to serve God, and to acknowledge that we are unprofitable servants. It expected men to be holy, and to know that they are sinners. Now it is different. Crowds of contented sinners are sung the praises of "human nature," and assured of God's exclusive love for it. The clergy flatter the people, indirectly of course, most indirectly. Naturalistic writers convince them that they are sex-ridden and self-seeking progeny of an apish beast. In the meanwhile, we are on our way towards a hell into which none but "God's noblest creation" will manage to enter.

It is quite evident that sense of proportion is not a common phenomenon. It seems to be a rare and difficult virtue. Neither "religion" nor "science" is sufficient guarantee against the ubiquitous folly of wrong estimation. To recognize both the greatness and the littleness of man, to see the broken image of his excellence in his sinful pride, and the evidence of his folly in his vaunted wisdom, to understand exactly how he is great and how he is little, seem to require a virtue dependent upon "supernatural light." It is indeed difficult to own that confession of sin is essential to righteousness, confession of ignorance to wisdom, recognition of weakness to power, the fear of hating to love. It is difficult to own that our freedom is in the knowledge of our bondage, our nobility in our knowledge of ourselves as creatures, our claim to a special position in the world, in our realization that we occupy no such position. The sin in us confounds our sense of proportion, so that we see great as little, and little as great. There is no more certain sign of sin than this. It is pride, folly, and ill-will rolled into one *massa corruptionis.*

3. *The Gospel of Jesus Christ*

It is a terrible thing that the Christians have turned the "Gospel of God" into an occasion of pride and folly. It is hard to imagine a pride more extreme than the conviction that the "last end" of the Incarnation is the deification of man. It is as though the Gospel were preached for the sole end of adding fuel to the already insufferable fire of self-love. "God loves me. God's Son died for me. God cares and provides for me. He forgives my sins and will raise me from the dead. He is my Father, and wills and does only what is good for me. . . . The so-called "Gospel religion" of the revivalists, and its more refined versions founded upon "The Fatherhood of God and the brotherhood of man," through their uncritical preoccupation with the problem of salvation, or of "brotherly love," have turned the Christian God into an idol whose sole function is to promote human happiness. It has become unthinkable that the Son of God should have sought to glorify God first, and to save sinners second; as though the salvation of the sinner, or his goodness, were not that he should honor and obey God the Creator of heaven and earth.

The anthropocentric interpretation of the "Gospel of Jesus Christ" is a gilded product of sin in the hearts and minds of the professed disciples of Jesus. It is a distortion of the theocentric religion of Jesus, turned into a celebration of the "infinite value of human personality." And yet—Jesus came preaching the kingdom of God, His sovereignty over man and nature, His power over Satan and his works, His outgoing love for the sinner, His justice and severity, His providence and impartial generosity. His parables extolled the excellence of God. His sayings described man's duty before God. His healings were done as acts of God. His dealings with men were inspired by the ultimate purpose of revealing a goodness peculiar to God. He was crucified by men who cared more for the Law and the Tradition, for the remunerative worship of the Temple, and for political peace, than for the Kingdom of God. He was raised from the dead by the love and power of God. He lived and died and rose from the dead—to the greater glory of God.

Indeed Jesus came calling sinners to repentance. And yet, what was this repentance, but that men should live under God, honoring, obeying, and serving Him! Is it not a perversion of His teaching to present Him as One who taught the love of God for men, without going on to state emphatically that this love became operative in men's recognition of God's "infinite perfections"? Surely, One who threatened sinners with the wrath of God, as well as declaring the forgiveness of God to them, cared more for the honor of God than for the "happiness of man." Unlike the friends of mankind and tender-minded universalists of our day, He did not shrink from the fact that those who do not honor and obey God must live in the hell of godlessness. Jesus came turning the hearts and minds of men towards God who is supremely excellent and worthy of man's "disinterested love" and ultimate devotion.

God whom Jesus loved and obeyed was God of nature as well as God of men. The student of the Gospels can hardly fail to realize that God whom Jesus sought to reveal to men filled the heavens and the earth with His glory. He made the sun to rise, the rains to fall, the winds to blow, the flowers to be clothed in beauty, the birds of the air to be fed, and the seeds to grow into trees or rich ears of corn. His parables, spoken to teach men about God, were saturated with God's glory revealed in nature as well as in the social life of men. The spontaneous and intelligent love of Jesus for those around Him was integral to that "disinterested love of God" which is impossible without proper regard for God's sovereignty over "universal Being." The compassion of Jesus for the "sheep without shepherd," or "the multitudes" of deeply miserable people around Him, was rooted in a vision of human life in its proper relation to God; and this compassion found its practical expression in His preaching that "the Kingdom of God is at hand."

Jesus' death upon the Cross is the Christian's ultimate symbol of the "disinterested love of God." Once again, how the Christians have perverted the "meaning of the Cross," through repeated failure to put first things first. "Christ died that we might be saved from sin and death. He gave His life a ranson for many." True. But how? Jesus was killed because He opposed those who dishonored God by making magic out of the Law, and idolatry out of the worship of the Temple; because He strove against those who offered the people a lucrative means of justification, bringing honor upon themselves rather than upon God. Jesus died because He upheld the "otherness" and sovereignty of God, and His freedom from the shackles which ecclesiastics seek to throw upon His hands. He was killed because He gave the glory to God. And it was thus that He is "our Savior." For to be delivered from sin and death is to worship God and to serve *Him*. It were indeed folly to pervert the life and work of Jesus to mean that God cares less for His glory than for the happiness of man, or that "God loves man" is the ultimate word of the Gospel of Jesus Christ. Jesus' God is Alpha and Omega. He is King in the heavens and upon the earth. Man is saved or becomes blessed when he honors, obeys, and serves God.

The willingness of Jesus to die in the service of God is the ultimate evidence of His vision of the primacy of God. It may well be that Jesus did not mount the Cross with any precise conviction as to what awaited Him beyond His death. It does not appear that His own destiny was a primary consideration during the ordeal of the last days. It is likely that He committed Himself to God and gave Himself up to His murderers. However, the impression is clear that the death of Jesus upon the Cross was and remains the triumph of the disinterested love of God over self-love. The readiness to die for the sake of God, to lose one's life according to the will of God, to honor and serve God who decrees one's death, are ultimate tokens of that love of Being in general which issues in the love of the neighbor, so that one is ready to die for him. Jesus died for the sinner. But He died for the love of God who is King over all. First the love of God; the love of men second. Such is the "order of love" according to the Son of God the Crucified.

The death of Jesus was a stumbling block to the Jews and foolishness to the Greeks. To this day, reason and conscience are uneasy at the suggestion that God had a part in it. The idol whom many worship in God's stead, who will not cause a single man to become unhappy, had of course no hand in it, for the simple reason that he does not exist. But God who established the course of events in this world so that nothing happens contrary to the "constitution" wherewith He governs the affairs and destinies of men, did most certainly will and decree the Cross of Jesus Christ. With a freedom from the conventions of human reason and conscience possible only for God, He permitted His Son to be killed by the ungodly. He thus repudiated once for all the proud thought of man that God's thoughts are his thoughts, and his ways are God's ways. He permitted the death of His Son, and thus exposed the terrible villainy of the human heart. Thus He convicted man of sin, leaving him without excuse. He dramatized unforgettably the selfishness and callousness which hold sway throughout this wide world, and emphasized infinitely the heinousness of sin by allowing it to destroy the righteous Man of Nazareth. (The Christians say He is the only sinless man that ever lived, and they may well be right.) He thus revealed man to himself as he really is in the depths of his heart and mind, and established the foundations of righteousness in repentance. The memory of the Righteous One soon coalesced with the vision of His resurrection from the dead, God's love for righteousness and His hatred of sin were made manifest, the Spirit of Christ came to dwell among the people, and God was vindicated in the repentance of sinners throughout the world, from India to Spain. Thus God was glorified among men, His Kingdom was revealed, and His last end in decreeing the death of His Son accomplished. Man the sinner has never ceased to become scandalized by the Cross, but the Spirit of God continues to strive with him to the end that he may understand, assent, and become blessed.

4. *Election and Predestination*

The death of the Son of God to the glory of God confronts us with election and predestination; for it was the consequence of a necessity wrought in the "constitution of the world." It was rooted in the creation and fall of man, in the Law and the Prophets, in the sin of Israel and in the hope of Israel, in the act of God whereby He was given the Spirit of God, the Spirit of understanding, obedience, compassion, and power. He was called, as were the patriarchs and the prophets, and He became the Head of the servants of God, the Head of the elect of God. He was chosen and called to manifest the glory of God in His life, death, and resurrection from the dead. He obeyed the call, and proceeded to do the will of God with a single-mindedness and steadiness which have won Him the title of "the Sinless One." He received His task, and accepted it with a readiness which reveals a perfect union of His will with the will of God. Thus He was elected to glorify God, and predestined to serve Him even unto death. God's eternal purpose of communicating His glory *ad extra*, and Jesus' obedience were two aspects of the same fact of His Sonship. His adoption and assent constituted a unity of act whereby He was the "Suffering Servant of God." As Edwards would have said: God did all, and Jesus did all. Jesus, who gave His life up to the glory of God, lived and acted as the Elect, the Predestinate, the Called of God. How unthinkable it is to have heard Him say: "I resent my election. I do not believe I was predestined and called to serve God. God owes my obedience to my free will. *I* have chosen to make my will to coincide with God's purposes. I shall have my reward according to my high merit. God shall keep me from evil and bless me with a happy life!" Jesus was blessed, not because He considered His freedom and virtue, but because He was the Prophet of God, chosen and called of God that He might honor and serve Him among men.

The doctrines of election and predestination were essential to the mind of the Protestant Reformation;

they were ultimate expressions of its theocentric religion. They are historic tokens of a religion in which the acts and purposes of God are primary. A man whose heart and mind are bent towards the knowledge of God and the service of God, gives his assent to the priority of God, of His will and of His glory. Fixing his attention upon the "perfections of God" revealed in nature and history, he is satisfied to consider that God is the ultimate Author of the careers and destinies which reflect His glory. He would rather that God be honored through His creation, than that *he* be independent of Divine decrees. He would rather know God's purposes, than have the freedom to follow his own desires. He would rather learn God's will, than be free to do his own. He would rather be elected by God to obey Him, than conceive of the glory of God as dependent upon his exercise of "free will." He would rather be predestined to serve God, than achieve virtue and merit through "free" choice of the good. He would rather be called of God, than be free to oppose His will and to hide His glory.

Martin Luther employed the doctrines of election and predestination as ultimate denials of justification by works. A man predestined for salvation is justified, most evidently, by God and not by his own works. Hence, any one who takes the doctrine of justification by faith seriously, who recognizes that it is God alone who can save man from sin-death, neither can nor will flinch before election and predestination, which destroy man's last pretensions and evasions. Such a man possesses the proper credentials to a realistic recognition of man's helplessness before sin and death, to a genuine knowledge of himself as a creature dependent upon his Creator, to wisdom, faith, and humility. The doctrine of predestination is the sober mind's confession that the known confronts us with the secret, the present with the past, the here with everywhere, the temporal with the eternal, the sinful with the Perfect, man and nature with God. It is the disillusioned man's last hope for life without death and righteousness without sin.

Lutheran piety, with its profound preoccupation with sin and salvation, emphasized the inner life of man. Calvinistic Protestantism has sought to turn men's attention to the "knowledge of God," to the honoring and service of God. Its tendency has been outward, towards an objective world and an objective Bible, towards understanding and practice. Edwards, trying to find "the distinguishing marks of a work of the Spirit of God," settled upon action in conformity to the will of God as the indispensable, visible, and definitive evidence of "holiness." The Calvinistic imaginaion, dominated by the wonders of God's works as told in the Old Testament as well as in the New, turning habitually to the contemplation of the "mighty acts" of God in nature as well as among the nations, conceived of God as "Infinitely the greatest and best of beings." "All things else," said Edwards, "with regard to worthiness, importance, and excellence, are perfectly as nothing in comparison to Him." Therefore, and reasonably enough, to the Calvinist, all things else, with regard to worthiness, importance, and excellence, were perfectly as nothing in comparison to the service of God. The consequent objectivity of Calvinistic piety led to a religion which is absolutely different from a religion of "good works." The Calvinist served God in order to honor Him, and not in order to receive the reward of His grace. The astonishing self-manifestations of God in nature and history, especially as revealed by the Old and the New Testaments, made it most obviously proper that man should attend to God, and not God to man. Not that God, who is "infinitely, eternally, unchangeably, and independently glorious and happy," *needs* man's honoring and service. Here again, Calvinistic sense of proportion makes all human presumption ludicrous. The honor and service which man offers to God are themselves "refulgences of Divine glory." They are creative acts of God, and not human mendings of Divine deficiency. They are signs of Divine favor which in no way circumscribe His freedom and sovereignty. The destiny of any given man, for all his zeal in piety, or for all of his many sins, remains a secret with God, unaltered and unalterable by human works. Hence man's last wisdom and duty are to commit his destiny into the hands of God, and to honor and serve

Him as required by the Word of God. Calvinistic piety is thus the virtual triumph of the love of God over human self-love and the anguish attendant upon it. It is the "disinterested love of God," which at once condemns man for his continued rebellion against the Determiner of Destiny, and delivers him from bondage to sin-death.

Such Calvinism was profoundly happy with predestination. It contemplated human life as wrought and guided by the hand of the Eternal, and set itself to do the day's work with a single-mindedness and courage possible only for those who lean upon "the Rock of Ages." It took its failures with a realism and sobriety given only to those who recognize that *God* cannot be defeated. The Calvinists lived and worked knowing that even their sins redounded to the glory of God through the manifestation of His justice, patience, wisdom, and forgiveness, and justified God who decreed them.

The crown of Protestant piety is the doctrine of "double election." The notion that God elects some for salvation and others for damnation, which even a theologian like Emil Brunner dismisses as a product of logic rather than piety, is the penultimate product of the Protestant spirit. However easily misunderstood (and it has been universally misunderstood!), it represents the virtual liberation of the religion from the anthropocentric perspective, and the delusion, magic, and idolatry it generates. It is the last assertion of God's ultimate freedom as He creates the world, a last terrible tribute to the facts of reprobation as known in this world, a last recognition that one's eternal destiny and one's present status before God are secrets known only to God. It is man's last avowal that the "communication *ad extra*" of God's internal glory, the "manifestation of his infinite perfections," whether in the good or the evil which life brings to man, even in the sin and death of man, is the "last end for which God created the world." The doctrine of double election, with the implied "willingness to be damned to the glory of God," are essential to Protestant piety. They are iron badges of the Protestant's wisdom, reverence for fact, disinterested love of truth, triumph over self-love in the disinterested love of God.

The Protestant is sinner among sinners. He does not *choose* "to be damned to the glory of God." His only hope, since he is in the Christian Church, is the Spirit of Him who preached the Kingdom of God and died that he might enter it. Hence, he can do no better than to pray that God give him "the mind of Christ."

Protestantism as described in this chapter is far more congenial to the contemporary mind than religion inspired by Catholic piety and authoritarianism, by eighteenth-century "faith in man," his "divine nature" and "free will," by nineteenth-century faith in progressive evolution, leading to an age of sinless and universal happiness in this world. Its tough-minded recognition of reprobation as rooted in the nature of things and man, its sober avowal of the multiplicity of ends in this world, its renunciation of the anthropocentric perspective, its passion for objectivity, its reverence for fact, its search for wisdom which can guide desire by the light of truth, make historic Protestantism a genuine religion for the contemporary man. When the latter understands the former and comes to appreciate its spirit, a primary condition for the revival of the Christian religion in our midst will have been fulfilled. Then he will learn to read the Bible, the Book written to the glory of God, with understanding and faith. He will learn to honor Him who accepted life and death in the service of God and man. He will then repent of his sins and pray that he might have the righteousness of God in Christ Jesus.

It is indeed true that justification by faith and not predestination is the original and primary doctrine of Protestant Christianity. None of the sixteenth-century reformers gave the latter the space and prominence suggested by this chapter. Nevertheless, any present day Protestant who is scandalized by this doctrine, and will have none of it, either is ignorant of Protestantism, or does not understand it, or does not approve of it. In any case, he is a man unworthy of his heritage, and a stumbling block to his neighbor.

The fact of evil has driven the contemporary man to a profound practical atheism. The only effective antidote to this his disease is a religion which acknowledges and teaches that the last end of creation is the glory of God, made manifest by both the good and the evil in this world; that man's good consists in the knowledge and service of God; and that this good is received, at least in the "Christian world," through Christ who loved God and not Himself.

Chapter Three

ON THE PROBLEM OF RIGHTEOUSNESS

A. ON THE PROBLEM OF SIN

1. Sin as Virtual Death. Critique of Moralism
2. Antidote to Inhumanity. The Nature of Compassion
3. The Problem of Social Sin

B. ON THE PROTESTANT LIFE

1. The Biblical Account of the Human Tragedy
2. The Power of the Cross of Jesus Christ
3. Obedience to God and the Service of God
4. Contemplation and Criticism in the Protestant Life

A. ON THE PROBLEM OF SIN

1. *Sin as Virtual Death. Critique of Moralism*

THE CONTINUED prevalence of "man's inhumanity to man" suggests that the problem of sin is rooted in the problem of life. Sin and death, which are the two foci of the tragedy of life, may well have a natural and indissoluble connection with each other, and it may be that an adequate understanding of this connection has important bearing upon the problem of the good life.

And yet, it has nowadays become a habit with our moralists to discourse upon the origins and nature of "moral evil" without giving much thought to the coexistence of sin and death in human life. Saint Paul's juxtaposition of "this body of death" and the "sin that dwelleth within me" does not seem to make sense to our moral analysts. They attribute sin to selfishness, ignorance, ill will, unimaginativeness, cultural and social conditions, and the like. It seems to them that men sin for one or more of these reasons (selected in number and order of importance according to the taste and insight of a given moralist), and then die, as a matter of course, some hoping for a future life, many content to cease being and becoming. Such is a basic assumption of contemporary ethical theory, which has become extremely dull and platitudinous.

It is improbable that mortality has no profound influence upon the conduct of men. The fear or anger of animals when confronted with the danger of death, the stiff fight they put up against the beast of prey or the astonishing swiftness with which they run away from it, are strong indication that life abhors death. The lively struggle for existence which sends animals in search of food and shelter, and provides them with instruments for acquiring and keeping the means of their livelihood, is loud declaration that the urge to maintain life and to avoid death plays a perennial role in animal life. "Beastliness," pouncing upon and throwing down, clawing and scratching, tearing and devouring, together with howling, roaring, and snarling, are parts of the frightful battle of life with death, the expressions of life in the valley of the shadow of death. Animals care whether they are dead or alive.

Man is an animal. He has the animal's urge to be and keep alive. He also searches for food and drink, fights those who stand in his way, and fortifies himself against the messengers of death: drought and pestilence, fire and the sword, and beasts of prey, human or nonhuman. He builds fortifications, invents weapons, and stands on guard. He seeks security and power in a social existence, sets up armies and governments, learns to exchange goods, competes and co-operates. The economic and political life of man is an extension of the struggle for existence. The shadow of death is cast upon it, from one end to the other.

The education of the youth has its primary effect in the fashioning of the "upstarts" in life according to the mind and heart of the community in which they exist, in moulding them into respectable and useful citizens. Writing and reading, arithmetic and "science," history and geography, and even literature and the arts, form character and prepare the young to promote the well-being of society as well as their own. The children sing, play, and study together, under the watchful eyes of good and dependable people. Thus they are made very much like each other and taught conformity to the mores and ideals of the community. Many of them attain civic sainthood by dying for the fatherland.

Religion is cultivated to the same end. "Vicars of Bray" act as promoters of public morality, and become willing instruments for the inculcation of principles and emotions useful for the good life as demanded by society. They ally themselves with "whatsoever king may reign," and champion the cause of law and order. Even when they are critical of the ways of the people, they protest solemnly their loyalty to the common good and happiness. Thus religion, in spite of the open secret of public indifference and hypocrisy, flourishes as a major instrument of social cohesion and common welfare.

Art throws in its share towards the "education of the

people." It celebrates the tastes of the community in music, the theatre, poetry, novels, biography, etc. It creates a "culture" which fortifies the emotional attachment of the people to the ways of the community. Certain styles of song and dance, writing and painting, cutting stones and erecting buildings, mould the feelings of the people and form their habitual likes and dislikes. They become integral to personality, and fix loyalty to the community in which they flourish. Once again, social unity and solidarity is enhanced, and can be exploited easily towards conflict with enemies within and without.

An original and permanent motif in the social life of man is the struggle for existence. Community life, even when seemingly irrelevant to the struggle of life with death, is permeated with the fear of frustration and the sin that flows from this fear as water from a fountain. Imagine human society without the shadow of death cast upon all life! Do angels buy and sell, marry and beget, go to school and play politicis, build houses and practice law or medicine, appoint judges, policemen, and mayors? Do they raise armies and fight battles, exploit and oppress their fellow angels, malign each other and thrive on scandal? Why is it that men have imagined them as harmless, serene, and contented; without fear, envy, or anxiety, without passion, hatred, or cruelty? Is it not because it is unthinkable that immortals should struggle and go mad? Lucifer and his hosts have always been strange monstrosities whose wickedness cannot be accounted for. The immortals have no good reason for sinfulness. They have no fear of starvation, deadly disease, murderous enemies, nature red in tooth and claw. Even if they hunger or have a headache, get cold or hot, or walk near a precipice, they are not-frightened. They have no real anguish, no terror, horror, or deadly despair. They are not hurt, vengeful, or cruel. They do not rob, kill, or commit adultery. They have no armies, prisons, or brothels. In short, they do not live as we live, nor do they die as we die.

Man's persistent anticipation of ultimate frustration is the source of that anguish which is the connecting link between sin and death. Selfishness and injustice, exploitation and oppression, originate in the doomed life of man, in his conscious or unconscious desperation. They are the the dumb and sullen protests of our life, symptoms of a hidden but potent rebellion against manifest destiny. Sin is the restless and persistent murmuring of the soul, the undercurrent of discontent and ill-temper with which it greets its end in an enduring world. It is rooted in the horrible intuition that nature's last word to man is "Nay," in the loss of faith and hope which are life's food and drink. It is diseased life.

Hurt and frustrated life is prone to sheer cruelty. Look at this man's ill-concealed, even though shamefaced, satisfaction at the news that a total stranger has just met his death; the more violent, the more exciting and gratifying. A "torch murder," an "axe murder," poisoning, strangulation, shooting: how dreadful, how gratifying! "News" for you! See him go around, listening to tales of other people's follies and failures. A man has been caught cheating, stealing, unfaithful to his wife; doing any one of a hundred things which could ruin his name and endanger his place among his fellow men: how terrible, how gratifying! Watch your mild and respectable subject maligning and backbiting: how cautious he is ("Not a word to anybody!"), how excited, how dreadfully satisfied! His voice sinks into a whisper, his eyes dilate; he gloats, and squirms, and apologizes, and protests sorrow and sympathy: all at once. He has been spared. The other has been taken. Aha! He is having his moment of triumph. Yea, vaguely but powerfully, he is having his revenge. Against whom? For what reason? To what end? It does not matter. His warped soul and bewildered mind are happy. Another has been tortured and frustrated. He is having his revenge against the world which has ordained his own failure, which threatens to undo him at any time. There is loss of life or fortune. He is still safe! "Thank my stars! I must be watchful. I must do my best to make myself secure against the cruelties of man and nature. I must stand on guard. I will not allow myself to be cast out like this poor devil, or to be destroyed like that consummate fool. I must play the game, I must outwit my fellow men; I must make friends and hold my enemies back; I must acquire power and destroy the destroyers. I must eat, drink and be merry, for tomorrow I die." Poor rebel! Poor sick soul! Poor sinner!

The usual target of moralistic shooting is selfishness. This vice is denounced from Protestant pulpits, week in and week out, as the great obstacle to peace and harmony among men. But quite clearly, selfishness is a general and ambiguous name for a multitude of sins, and cannot be exorcised by exhortation. A child refusing to share its ball or doll with another is selfish; so is a boy who refuses to give one of four apples in his bulging pockets to a friend, a young man who refuses to interrupt a tennis game in order to run an errand for his mother, a young lady who will not take part in a play unless she is given a major part, a woman who demands special treatment for her child in school, a man who seeks to ruin his neighbor's business by underselling and maligning him. Now, what is selfishness? Fear of losing one's ball or doll, desire to fill one's belly to the full, preference for a tennis game to pleasing one's mother, desire for applause and popularity, love of one's child, the will to succeed in one's business. The motives behind "selfishness" are almost as numerous as the selfish acts men do. Fear or physical urge, desire for power and security, for public admiration and respect are all sources of selfishness. Selfishness cannot be combatted effectively through the moralist's repeated denunciations of it and his pleas for "unselfishness." The connection between the general vice of selfishness and its particular acts is so vague and obscure, the particular causes of selfish acts so "natural" and constraining, and the ends sought by them so desirable, that ordinary preaching against selfishness is next to futile. Hence, the common antidote for it is not so much a general sense of its wickedness as painful awareness of the evils produced by its several acts. These evils, anticipated or actual, lead people to guard against opposition to the self-love of others. "Selfishness" is in short neither fundamental enough in human nature, nor particular and definite enough as a vice, to lend itself to proper treatment by pulpit orators. It is rather a symptom or a series of symptoms which require further diagnosis and point to vices beyond themselves.

Ill will is a step further removed from the roots of behavior in the human soul. It appears in a hundred guises when particular objectives are frustrated or are in danger of frustration. Men cross our purposes, and become objects of our ill will. They threaten us with the loss of our good name, or our comforts, or even our livelihood. They bite us and they sting us, to our face and behind our backs. With them or away from them, we feel insecure. We suspect them of hypocrisy towards us, and treat them hypocritically. We suspect them of readiness to rejoice in our disgrace and failure, and proceed to be pained by their success and gratified by their frustration. And since where there is a will there is also fear of others, our trust in our fellow men is always tempered by ill will, which becomes rooted in our nature as a permanent part of it. Hence this vice cannot be dealt with effectively without insight into our purposes and their roots in the necessities of body and soul, into emotions aroused by failure, and into the role which reason and imagination play in the making of our volitions. Ill will also is neither fundamental enough to be "the root of all evil," nor particular enough to be a fit subject of effective exhortation against it. It is mitigated and sometimes overcome when men recognize it as a source of danger and harm in their relations with their fellow men.

The common and effective means of combatting evil impulses lies in the slow and painful discovery that *often* "no good comes out of evil." The repeated returns of the evils we do to others upon our own heads, the enemies we make by opposing too obviously the wishes and interests of others, the dangers we run into when we arouse the common resentment of our frightened neighbors, teach us minimum decency and turn us into respectable people. Moralistic exhortation is at best vague and general reminder that if we want peace and security in the community in which we live, we had better behave well. But the application of our "moral principles" to particular situations is made as we employ our imagination and good sense towards recognizing that virtue is *often* profitable. Our "goodness" is primarily a product of social necessity co-operating with reason in the service of self-love.

Those who attribute immorality to ignorance and unimaginativeness deserve more serious attention than the ordinary pedlar of moral platitudes. Given the natural self-love of men which produces the moral evils in our midst, an increase of insight into the consequences of these in conflict and suffering is a source of considerable decency and co-operation among men. A man who realizes that anger and envy will antagonize his neighbor will control himself often, and reap the rewards of his patience and goodwill in continued peace and comfort. One who is tempted to assault or steal is benefitted by a mental image of a policeman or a prison. If he is a "normal man," willing "to live and let live," his reason will be quite helpful in keeping him from doing evil and suffering harm. Wickedness is often stupid, and intelligence is a good antidote to it. And yet, reason and imagination which remain insensible to the roots of sin in self-love, and uncritical of the common "pursuit of happiness," are incapable of any radical influence upon the selfishness, ill will, injustice and the like which find secure lodging in the heart of the most clever man, yea, which even increase his wickedness. The ultimate answer to those who conceive of prudence as the solution of the ethical problem is the evil we do when we would not do it, and the good we would do, but do not. Rationalism is too naïve and superficial.

Neither the moralists' exhortations, nor the rationalists' arguments, nor society's coercions, are basic cures for "man's inhumanity to man." The diabolical manifestations of sin in our common life today are due to a determined effort of the contemporary man to live and act as though the anguish of life before death were unreal. This is the essence of our secularism and the root of the new terrors which sin has produced in our day. We are engaged in a concerted effort to overlook the "tragic sense of life." Much of our social life is an attempt at escaping self-awareness, at filling our days with busy-ness and pleasure which turn our minds and hearts from time and transience, from self-conscious life's horror of death. Business, profession, or politics; the arts, and the sciences, and the sports; our endless conversations on selfless topics,—allow us minimum of reflection upon the "meaning of life" or the relation of our life to God's eternity. Thus we refuse to "consider," to take account of man's true place in a vast and enduring world. We ignore our life, and woo and love the lifeless. But life is not cheated easily. Its struggle for existence continues as a sinful thing. When the soul's anguish is ignored and even ridiculed, when men seek to forget themselves by turning their attention to the many things in the world and seek happiness in the knowledge and enjoyment of them, when they make the arts occasions for losing themselves in one sensual experience or another, when they go so far as to allow human relations to degenerate into mutual help in self-forgetfulness, they become enslaved to their world and live in sin. The perennial efforts of men to hush up the soul's protest against time and its passing, through union and fusion with the not-self in and around them, is contrary to their nature, unhealthy, and sinful. A scorned and neglected self-consciousness takes its revenge by making us callous and cruel. Whether it skulks as indifference to our neighbor or recoils and strikes back as selfishness and ill will, it becomes the "root of all evil." It turns conscious life into a senseless kicking against the pricks, fills it with fear and suspicion, irritates it into injustice and cruelty, and turns us into sinners, respectable or otherwise.

Your harmless pleasure seeker, the "hail-fellow-well-met" sort of person who "wouldn't hurt a fly," shows repeated signs of petty self-preference which set up a barrier between him and others. He wants to be praised a little louder than his neighbor; he would be more important, more sought after, more honored than the next man. He is insulted by criticism, crushed by neglect, and infuriated by another's selfishness. It is necessary to humor, pacify, and flatter him; by all means, to treat him better than the men to his left or right. His friends treat him with the deference due him, and save themselves much unnecessary trouble. He is now a man with an "ego," thoroughly "human," and equally "difficult," both to himself and to others.

The poison within him begins to work violently when he is confronted with a threat to his life or the way he lives it. A cold shiver runs through him, and all the little hairs on his body raise their empty heads in pitiful fright. Somebody is threatening his good name. Another is a successful competitor in business or profession. A third is a clever politician, and is running away with his neighbors' good graces. The strangers within the gates, men of another social or economic group, of another race, religion, or nationality, are constant, even when veiled, threats to his power, security, happiness, and even existence. Nobody is to be trusted absolutely, nobody is to be befriended overmuch, nobody is to be given a chance to "do him dirt."

Such self-centered fear is transmuted easily into injustice and cruelty. Self is set up against other self and the world at large. Its affirmation of the life within is transformed into a negation of the life in others. It is ready to resist, to strike, and to destroy. Success is attained at the expense of others' failure, power at the expense of others' weakness, security at the expense of others' insecurity. Might learns to ignore right, and injustice becomes an accepted instrument of success. A profound indifference towards the unfortunate becomes a permanent part of life, and oppression thrives as a "natural" means of "keeping on top." "It is too bad," says the prosperous and secure man, and turns his head around to forget the "natural" evils and unpleasantnesses around him. And if his unhappy neighbor were to protest and threaten, he would call the police, have the man tried, condemned, and thrown into the jail: out of the way. Our egoist may well be a mild and decent fellow. But he will fight his enemies, real and imaginary, to the finish. If necessary, men are clubbed, gassed, and shot at. They kill one another, and life is turned into hell.

The intelligence and will attached to a diseased soul endow its works with a demonic quality which is absent from the destruction wrought by the wildest beast. Man the sinner is alone in his ill will and hatred, in his ferocity inspired by bad conscience, in his suicidal desperation as he destroys life and limb. The beastliness of the beast is natural; the inhumanity of man is diabolical. The former is God's gift to the animal; the latter is the obliteration of the image of God in man. The former preserves a beast's life; the latter destroys a man's soul and turns his life into damnation. When man sins, all creation stand aghast and marvel at his wickedness. The world groans, the devils crouch together and shiver, the angels flee to heaven and gather around the throne of God. But for His grace which comforts us and gives us hope, we could not endure this hell of man's sin against man—no not for one moment.

2. *Antidote to Inhumanity. The Nature of Compassion*

The first antidote to "man's inhumanity to man" is an unflinching confrontation of the tragedy of life. Unless men are adequately impressed with the pathos of their existence as human beings, unless they place these three-score-and-ten years in their proper setting in eternity, unless they know the ultimate hopelessness inspired by the vanity of all things in the world, unless they are chastened and sobered by the flow of time which bears all things away—unless they allow their mortality to pierce their souls and hurt them at the very roots of life, they are without a radical treatment for the disease of sin. The tragic sense of life is the serum which flows through the soul, and makes it capable of resisting, though never too successfully, the folly and madness of inhumanity.

The Christian Gospel of deliverance from sin and death presupposes the tragic sense of life. The doctrine of Original Sin gives it a place of honor in Christian theology. The great devotional literature of the Church, from Augustine's *Confessions* to Law's *Serious Call,* is saturated with it. The historic asceticism in the Christian Church was often inspired by it and gave it dramatic expression in the privations men imposed upon themselves. The people's clothing and food, their prejudices against song and drama, their Sunday observance, etc., were direct or indirect tributes to it. In fact a major distinguishing mark of Chrisitan piety was "godly sorrow" dominated by the memory of the Crucified who died because of human sin. The historic Christian Gospel was preached to a people in the valley of the shadow of sin and death.

But Christianity has all too often muffled the voice of despair within by unseasonable and noisy celebration of the "Gospel faith." The Protestants of today run away from "pessimism" as from a plague. They prefer to speak of the love of God, of the excellence of man as revealed by Jesus of Nazareth, of the hope of perfection and eternal life given us by the "Gospel of God." But they will say as little as possible about the tragedy of the human situation which gives point and meaning to the Gospel. The people are constantly called upon to look at the good and pleasant sides of life, to be confident, hopeful, and joyful. Thus the Christian religion is turned into a colossal conspiracy to turn men's minds away from the anguish of life and to make them at home in this world and happy while life lasts.

This fact is at least a partial explanation of secularism and materialism as we find them in "western civilization." There is a real connection between a sunnyminded Christianity and the love of the world which characterizes our society. There is also a real connection between the loss of the perception of the world as "the valley of the shadow of death," and the systematic and destructive exploitation of man and nature in the western world. Optimistic religion, secularism, and exploitation, all attained at the expense of the tragic sense of life, are happy bedfellows and permanent friends to each other. Justice, mercy, kindness, humanity, helpfulness are products of that wisdom which nourishes itself upon the intuition of the "vanity of the world." When this intuition is darkened, there is nought but injustice and cruelty, at best veiled by sentimentalism and hypocrisy. A good case could be made for the contention that a light-headed and joy-dispensing Christianity has accentuated the curse of callousness in our western civilization. Self-seekers, exploiters, despisers of men, and enemies of justice, have been preached the gospel of the goodness of God and received the tacit blessing of clerics. The one institution whose duty it is to inject humility and sobriety into the human heart, to mitigate men's lust for the treasures of this earth, to discourage their bid for power over their fellow men, and to strike at the roots of sin and suffering in the love of things rather than of men, has prostituted itself and encouraged the self-love of men by picturing God and nature as instruments of their happiness in this world and in the next. This is the great folly of Christianity which has made us the laughingstock of the heathen and the wiser atheists in our midst.

A Christianity without the tragic sense of life is salt

without savor. It has no important contribution to make to the "ethical problem" of our day. It exhorts the people to "follow Jesus"; it challenges them to live by "the teachings of Jesus"; it commends "ethical idealism," praises "reverence for personality," and promises an "abundant life" to those who believe in God and love their neighbor. It speaks, volubly or threateningly, of goodness and selfishness, of justice and injustice, of co-operation and competition, of war and peace. But such moralism remains pointless and ineffective. In spite of the occasional enthusiasm it arouses, even when it pricks the conscience and presents the mind with frightful pictures of probable consequences of sin, it lacks the power to produce significant action. Since it neither is based upon a proper analysis of sin nor issues in realistic analysis of concrete "injustices"; since it claims for the teachings of Jesus an authority which they no longer possess; since it is determined to minimize the foundations of the good life in *via crucis*—it remains much smoke with little fire. It frequently degenerates into a teaching of platitudes which are tolerated because of their harmlessness and enjoyed when presented with enthusiasm and wit. But the very people for whom it is intended, those participating consciously in the "sins of society," brush it off their minds as so much dust off a wooden chair.

Hence there is a growing school of Protestant "realists" who recognize the futility of moralistic exhortation. They are painfully aware of how good thoughts and sentiments evaporate in the heat of "social and economic realities" where coercion and threat of coercion are ubiquitous instruments of stability and change. Sunday-morning idealism is poor soap for washing the deep and oily stain of sin in our industrial society, with its holding companies, absentee stockholders, managers whose one thought is profit, workers who must organize and threaten disaster before they can have security and make a decent living. Petty merchants, dealers in the thousand and one "goods" we hardly need or want, caught in the whirlpool of an acquisitive society, have to carry on a struggle for existence in which decency and ruthlessness are mixed together as required for the ultimate and necessary purpose of profit. General pleas for unselfishness and co-operation are cheap and worthless medicine for the social disease of our day. Our "realists," being aware of the "social struggle," participate in the economic conflicts around them and try to throw their weight on the side of the underprivileged and the exploited. They find the seeds of economic distress and war on the soil of our "acquisitive society," and advocate a co-operative or socialistic society as the solution of our problems. In the meanwhile, they plead for justice and decency in economic behavior in concrete terms of hours and conditions of work, for a decent wage and security against unemployment, for methods of checking the profiteering of the powerful who provide the people with their "living."

There can be little doubt that these advocates of "social justice" are more intelligent and serious than the glib-tongued dispensers of moral ideals who will not come near the fire of the economic conflict in our midst. But their contribution to our ethical problem remains doubtful. It operates as a minor addition to the forces of the underprivileged. It becomes a negligible part of a conflict carried on the level of unqualified self-interest. Thus religion becomes self-identification with those fighting for a larger share of the world's goods. It is often heroic and self-sacrificing. But it is not necessarily Protestant, because its analysis of sin stops short of adequate insight into its sources in the anguish of life and its resultant worldliness. It offers no profound critique of the self-love which is the moral foundation of our "acquisitive society." It overlooks consistently the probability that a co-operative society based upon a secular conception of the "common good" will be fundamentally incapable of coping with the roots of sin in life's struggle against death. Its vision of a better social order may well be correct. Its participation in the social struggle invests it with a strong note of authenticity and pertinence to our time. It certainly is a standing rebuke to the complacency of the sermonizing moralist. But its indifference to the metaphysic of life makes it insufficient as Protestantism for our time. Its contribution to the social struggle, for all the light it throws upon contemporary sin and the moral seriousness it inspires, can hardly be the fulfillment of the task of religion in our day.

Neither moralistic exhortation nor participation in the social struggles fulfil the primary function of religion. As moralists we must have principles and ideals; as sincere and intelligent men we must seek to make proper use of them in human relations. But religion is another matter. Its peculiar and indispensable function is to place human life in its proper setting in time and eternity. Its business is to bring men to themselves, to make them face themselves as centers of self-conscious life confronted with ultimate frustration, as sojourners upon this earth who know not whence they come and where they go; in short as mortals. It is the duty of religion to keep men from the terrible folly of turning aside from the anguish of life, of impersonalizing themselves in mindfulness of the thousand things around them; to emphasize, to dramatize, to celebrate the vanity of secularism, materialism, and all effort to find satisfaction in the possession and enjoyment of things. "Vanity, vanity, all is vanity," is a refrain which religion must sing, murmur, and shout, day in and day out. Religion must act as a constant deterrent of the mad passion for power and possession which flourishes through our common effort to overcome our creatureliness. This was the wisdom in the otherworldliness of historical Christianity which is scorned habitually and senselessly in our day. Devotional writers like the author of *Theologia Germanica,* Thomas à Kempis, Richard Baxter, and William Law were far more intelligent and wiser than the light-headed and light-hearted life-affirmers of our time. They knew the sobering, chastening, grace-giving influence of proper attention to the tragedy of human existence in this world. They knew that charity, compassion, kindness and the like which mitigate the ruthlessness and cruelty of men are rooted in a lively vision of the brevity and the necessary incompleteness of this our life. They knew that selfishness and oppression are fruits of men's permanent tendency to ignore our common destiny which turns everything into nothing. They mixed their polemics against "the love of money" with protests against the "love of the world" because they knew that the two go together; for the love of earthly treasures is indifference to death and the sin it generates.

The tragic sense of life acts as a purifying influence in human relations. When it becomes integral to self-consciousness, it generates a species of compassion which acts as a powerful antidote to selfishness. This compassion must be distinguished from pity and even sympathy which appear in the presence of particular events of pain and suffering. It is essentially different from that "being sorry" which is felt when an animal or a person is hurt. Its relation to pity is akin to the relationship between "true virtue" and "natural virtue." As, in Edwards' language, "true virtue" is a "new principle" or "holy disposition," while "natural virtue" is an extension of "self-love," so, compassion is a peculiar disposition of the self arising from the tragic sense of life, and must be distinguished from pity which depends upon vicarious suffering in the presence of the pain of another. It is anguish "in general," a principle which is prior to and the ground of any particular act of compassion. It belongs to the metaphysic of life and operates as the spirit of righteousness opposing itself to sinful flesh. As the latter underlies the self-centered life, compassion becomes a new foundation for life which has its center in God who transcends all centers and reveals their proper places in the world. It is a new standpoint which changes our perspective and gives us a new vision of the forms and relations of the things around us. It makes the heart-mind sensitive to colors and dimensions, to lights and shadows, to depths and intensities, which evade completely the blindness of self-love. It opposes the motives and interests of self-love with others inspired by ends and purposes other than our own. The thrust of self-love is repeatedly inhibited and redirected by a lively perception of the life-history of other beings. A new "feeling for others," a new understanding of others, a new benevolence towards others, act as antidotes to the aggressiveness, thoughtlessness, carelessness, callousness, crudity, vulgarity, bumptiousness, pettiness, "cussedness," vengefulness, and plain sadism which infest our common life and make it to stink to high heaven. The amount of irritation, pain, and suffering caused by the blind and senseless stinging administered by self-love, in every city, town, and village, wherever two and three are gathered together, over the whole surface of this wide world, is something that staggers the imagination and makes one abysmally sad. More nerves are distraught, more minds warped, and more hearts broken by the little stupidities of self-love than by its "blameworthy" wickedness. Compassion is the basic element of the deep decency which alone can counteract the poison which a diseased life generates and pours into all that come in contact with it.

The ethical mission of the Protestant religion today is to turn contemporary sense of vanity into an occasion of compassion instead of worldliness and its callousness. This means first of all a profound reorientation in religion itself. Instead of being a stubborn and dogmatic optimism, our religion has to appropriate the despair and hopelessness of the modern mind. Before it sets out to give people faith and hope, it has to drink deep of the cup of contemporary anguish. It has to improve upon the pessimism of the atheist by teaching him to face the tragedy to life in all its devastating power. It has to keep him from trying to escape it by endless preoccupation with the things around him. It is the task of religion to make people stop and consider, to sit down and be quiet; to think of time, of being born and dying, of ages past and ages to come, of the veil of insignificance which covers every accomplished end and long besought triumph. It is the task of religion to bring men to their senses.

The ethical problem is still the problem of wisdom: that wisdom which resists the aggressive impulses in us; which would rather lose than fight and make a noise; which would rather take the second or tenth place than push and knock down; which would rather be slapped than slap, rather be maligned than malign, rather be called a fool than call some one else a fool; which can see through success, power, domination, riches, honor, glory, and all things men seek after, and recognize them as rubbish and rot. But how can such wisdom be acquired except through the anguish of confrontation with the Eternal?

The wise or compassionate man is in this world, but he is not of the world. He goes about doing the day's work, receiving the joys and sorrows it brings, loving the good and hating the evil as nature prescribes. But his sense of vanity acts as a continuous deterrent to giving his heart over to anything in heaven or on earth. He cares, and he does not care. He wants, and he does not want. He fights, and he does not fight. He wins, and he does not win; he loses, and he does not lose. He rejoices, and he does not rejoice; he suffers, and he does not suffer. He is a slave, and he is free.

Our crude and thoughtless search for happiness in things which we must soon leave behind, our trampling upon our own souls and the souls of others as we rush headlong after the objects of our desire, our ill-conceived and ill-considered ambitions, our little and large inhumanities as we muzzle our conscience and suppress our heart, all these are the fruits of a radical abuse of life through the cumulative folly of unreflectiveness. Compassion is found among the wise who have learned of the vanity of life through the repeated turnings of joy into sorrow and of life into death. These wise people look at us with understanding eyes, tolerate our vulgarity and inconsiderateness, smile at our pompous self-assertions, step aside as we go forth to win and to dominate. They find joy in their compassion for us and sorrow in our foolish lust for things which are soon consumed by moth and rust. They are the authors of the quiet decencies which mitigate the conflict of life with life and provide relief from the irritations which self-love administers upon oneself and others.

3. *The Problem of Social Sin*

The petty immoralities of life are overtones of that fear of frustration which finds more obvious expression in the economic struggle. The little selfishnesses which mar our personal contacts are excrescences of a larger and unashamed selfishness which dominates the struggle for food, shelter and security. Hence, the areas of life in which self-love turns into selfishness most readily and dramatically is that of the scramble for the necessities of life. Here men are "out for themselves," and "nobody blames them." Here they must succeed, by foul means or fair. They must make profit, and receive the reward of their labor. Men would live and eat, rather than be just and kind. They would have power rather than virtue, security rather than benevolence. Hence it is on the level of economic life that self-love becomes a steady source of inhumanity.

Economists, sociologists, statesmen must deal with the concrete problems of economic and social amelioration as presented by specific and often intricate situations. Responsible citizens also have the duty of making full use of their opportunities towards the same ends, with maximum attention to definite problems of economic relations as represented by employer and employee, industry and agriculture, production and distribution. A primary task of religion as such with regard to social problems is to keep the earning of bread from turning into an occasion of "dog eat dog." Instead of occupying itself with "high ideals" which seem to have no observable relevance to the "making of a living," religion should present the latter as a part of life's battle with death. An unabashed recognition of the "economic basis of society" as a matter of immediate concern for religion, and an intelligent effort to define its relationship to man's anticipation of ultimate frustration, cannot but have a salutary effect by injecting wisdom and charity into the all-influential concern with "living." Let men labor for their bread, as they indeed must; but let them do it with the understanding that the food they eat is not the bread of eternal life, and the drink they drink is not the "medicine of immortality." The "fight for life" is carried on by sinners as though it were a fight for life without death; hence much of their ungodly zeal whereby they hurt each other and deprive others of the "necessities of life." It is the task of religion to celebrate the vanity of this dying life and to mitigate the cruelties which the struggle for it generates. A heart aware of the ultimate emptiness threatening us is a poor neighbor to a belly filled at the expense of inhumanity.

The social struggle in its present form and extent is not a necessary consequence of self-love. *Our* selfishness is a perverted expression of life's love for our and others' being. When reason and imagination transform the will to live into rebellion against anticipated death, the love of life degenerates into the love of the world, into a love of things above the love of men, and the foundations of injustice and social conflict are established. Thus men learn to ignore the anguish of life within them, and self-love is perverted into acquisitiveness. A life doubly frustrated both in its confrontation with death and in men's stubborn thoughtlessness, becomes insane and seeks fulfilment in the superfluities offered by the world. Denied its urge for being, it turns to the futility of striving after an abundance of perishable goods and a maximum of an impermanent security. Acquisitiveness and the lust for power are thus the fruits of life's desperation. "I may not live long; so, I will live well. I will surround myself with all the worldy goods I can acquire, and I will be merry (some call it 'happy') until I die. I shall become as powerful as possible, and defend myself against all my enemies. I shall make up for my mortality by making this life as enjoyable and satisfactory as possible. If necessary, I shall war against my fellow men. I shall have and enjoy plenty of everything. Thus I shall quiet the anguish in my soul. I shall live happily, though not "ever after." I shall achieve a maximum of power, I shall become superior in wealth and culture. Then I shall be able to despise and laugh at those less fortunate than myself. I shall be a king, yea a god,—for one day. If God's eternity is not for me, I shall emulate His power, sovereignty, and worshipfulness. Men shall speak of me with respect. They shall fear me. They shall honor me. I shall be a god to them—until I die."

The roots of men's inordinate desire for power and possessions are symptoms of a terrible malady caused by human maladjustment to nature. The human psyche is in permanent rebellion against man's place in nature. It cannot be content with life and death as prescribed by nature. Hence it develops predatory tendencies. It seeks to assume an importance it does not have. Hence it swells up with pride and tries to swallow the world. It is hurt with nature's indifference to its destiny. Hence it takes matters into its own hands and tries to achieve divine glory. It seeks to dominate, enslave, and exploit. Neither man nor nature is spared in its pursuit of self-aggrandizement, and our world is filled with evil and ugliness. Like a tyrant upon an unsteady throne, man despoils nature and oppresses his fellow men, while life lasts and the sword dangling overhead is still attached to the roof of time.

Inequality and injustice as known and practised among men enter into the world with "the Fall of Man," with man's rebellion against his creaturely destiny. It is folly to attribute them to struggle for existence as known among animals who will not fight and tear unless hungry or afraid. Hence it is also folly to try eliminating them by satisfying men's need for food and shelter. No "social change" will bring about the cessation of the *human* "struggle for existence"; for this struggle continues endlessly when the belly is full and there is a roof over one's head.

The roots of exploitation and oppression in our midst are in a spiritual malady which is peculiar to man and goes deeper than its expressions in any given pattern of social and economic behavior. It goes deeper than the processes of reason, will, or emotion, into man's problem of his destiny. Hence it is the awful responsibility of religion to counteract it and its product of lust for power which is by far the most potent cause of injustice and suffering among us. It is the indispensable task of religion to expose the folly of "the will to power," to declare the perfidy of a world which promises happiness proportionate to possessions, to pacify the ambitious and aggressive, to teach the sobriety and moderation which issue from the anguish of life and its sense of vanity. It is the function of religion to tackle the lunacy which makes men oppress and murder for the sake of trinkets which the beasts know better than to want or treasure, to put sense into the heads of would-be gods and Bonapartes who strut around in every village or hamlet in this wide world. This is the most subtle, the most difficult, the most discouraging task possible. But it is the task of religion: one which cannot possibly be fulfilled without proper attention to the metaphysical struggle of life against death and the related metaphysical problem of man's relation to the Eternal.

B. ON THE PROTESTANT LIFE

1. *The Biblical Account of the Human Tragedy*

Recent revival in theology and theological preaching is evidence of a renewed recognition that the ethical and the metaphysical problems belong together. For theology is after all metaphysics in which man's relationship to the Eternal occupies a prominent position. In theology the problems of sin and death are linked together and studied in relation to God the eternal Creator and sovereign Providence. Theological preaching is preaching in which men are led to meet their God and to consider their lives in the light of God. When man thinks before God there is theology. When he is made to listen to the "Word of God" there is preaching. But to listen and to think *sub specie Dei* is to consider sin and death in relation to the Eternal: and this is the special province of religion. Religion has no contribution to make to the "ethical problem" unless it presents the latter in relation to sin-death and God the Lord of Life. Hence, "religious ethics" is ethics in which moral evil is referred to the sin of rebellion against God, the Author of life and death, and righteousness is recognized as obedience to Him. Christian preaching, Christian theology, Christian ethics are preaching, theology, ethics in which sin and death are considered in the light of the Gospel of the crucified and risen Christ, which is also the "Gospel of God."

The source of theological preaching in the Protestant churches must remain the Bible. For it is the Bible where human life is viewed persistently and with utmost eagerness in the light of the sovereign God. The Biblical Deity is the Creator, the King and Judge, the Determiner of Destiny. To face Him is to face the Author of life and death, the King who has the underived right to demand absolute obedience, the Judge who is at once just and merciful, the Origin of the goods and evils which come upon the people. He is greater by far than all His creatures, and one and alone in His right to make His honor and glory the supreme end of His government of the world. Hence He is the Object of man's constant attention, and the Source of all his fears and hopes. The Bible is the Book of God and man, the "Word of God" to men who had the wisdom and humility to recognize that their destiny rests in the hands of One who is above them and over against them, causing good and evil, life and death, according to a constitution He has pleased to establish and to publish in the Law, and to a purpose which has its ultimate end in the manifestation of His glory of wisdom, justice and mercy to the people. The whole life of man—sickness and health, poverty and riches, war and peace, the blessings and curses of nature, life and death, celebrated with utmost simplicity and honesty,—are contemplated as acts of God. God is everywhere in the Bible, as the Hero of the story, the Speaker of the Word and the Doer of the deed; as the indispensable and inescapable Being whom men fear and love, honor and disobey, forsake and cleave to, trust and distrust, and reckon with at all times. The historians and the lawgivers, the prophets and priests, the poets and wise men who contributed to the making of the Old Testament remain the supreme exponents of theocentric religion.

Hence the Biblical material, even when concerned with situations which are hardly relevant to contemporary life, has a peculiar quality which makes it conducive to a strange reflectiveness and sobriety. The Bible is strange as life is strange; similarly familiar, moving, scandalous, unbelievable, obvious, profound, platitudinous, thought-provoking, real and unreal, consistent and inconsistent, pleasant and unpleasant, comical and tragic: the supremely faithful portrait of life. Like good and evil, sin and righteousness, life and death, it is plain as one's nose, and yet points consistently to a mystery, a veiled truth which is the perennial source of human restlessness. Its very earthiness and preoccupation with the concrete, pervaded by an elemental intuition of time and transiency, of dependence and indebtedness, of a secret and a problem, make it revelation, both mystery and Truth. "The Word of God" was spoken to a people whose honesty remains a miracle of the human heart. Hence also, their Book remains the Word of God to a world given to evasion and dishonesty. It remains the supreme instrument of self-criticism and the source of the Light which comes from God and reveals Him to the sons of sin and death.

In minimizing the tragic sense of life, contemporary Protestantism has done severe violence to the Bible which purports to be the Word of God to a people who, above all other peoples, knew their need of God; who lived in the valley of the shadow of death, well acquainted with sin, suffering, and destruction; who waited eagerly upon the Determiner of their destiny, ready to hear His judgments, statutes, and ordinances, searching their past and looking into their future, with repentance, fear, and hope. They were a people who had known bondage in Egypt, sin and death in their "wanderings," oppressions and deliverances when there was no king in Israel, humiliation under the Syrians, devastation under the Assyrians, and exile under the Babylonians. They were scattered over the face of the earth and ate their bread in bitterness, being at the mercy of those who ruled over them. They suffered much and understood much. Thus they became a light to the nations. We turn the light they gave us into darkness when we read their Book only to fortify our complacency. In doing so, we are not wise. A religion which shelves our despair with sin-death takes away our first reason for sobriety and humility. It blinds our eyes to our true humanity, to our true equality as those who need God, to our true brotherhood in our common need for righteousness and life. Having despised our need, such religion turns our faith into an "intellectual assent" and our hope into a vague and uninterested anticipation, and thus destroys the seeds of love in the human soul.

Protestant preaching in our day has suffered greatly by presenting the Bible as the *magna carta* of optimism. It has sought to make the Bible a gospel of man's security in the world. It has sought to deal with the unbelief and pessimism of the day by insisting that human life is in the hands of a kindly and indulgent Providence. It has largely ignored the somber and disquieting aspects of the Biblical message, especially as seen in the trials and sufferings of the Hebrew people. It has set aside the warnings written large across the history of the people of Israel, in favor of a breezy religion of Divine generosity which is supposedly evangelical but is really a supreme product of human complacency and idolatry. It has sought to preach a gospel of love without paying serious and sincere attention to the pathos of human life as described by the Bible; and thus it has lost the whole point and significance of "the Gospel of Jesus Christ the Son of God."

The terrible thing about Protestant preaching today is the constant insinuation that we do not *need* God.

High and hopeful views of man and nature have come to mean that the goodness and love of God are things we possess rather than need. When the cynical and pessimistic modern complains of the vanity of life, of the cruelty and low-mindedness of men, of the indifference of nature to the life and welfare of man, the preachers hasten to present the "other side of the picture," and the controversy ends in an apparent "draw" which satisfies none but those who wish to be comfortable and happy at all costs. They point to this and to that and say: "Lo God is here, lo God is there"; while the red-eyed unbeliever sees nothing but this and that! Such a "doctrine of the immanence of God," set up against contemporary naturalism, is the antithesis of the Biblical conviction that God is man's need and not his possession. The Biblical "hope" is inseparable from the Biblical cry for God. Similarly, any optimism *today* has to go hand in hand with the modern man's perceptions of the shadows drawn across the light of life. Any religion which consists of "glad tidings of great joy," without proper regard for "the face of covering that covereth all peoples, and the veil that is spread over all nations," is not Biblical and not a religion for the contemporary man.

Biblical religion is not a compromise between pessimism and optimism. It is a stranger to the contemporary religion which sets itself to make faith in God, or man, or nature, a conviction that as a matter of fact human life is a happy and hopeful affair. Biblical faith is not an eyepiece which makes the black look white, or the woeful blessed. It arises from confrontation with sin and death, and not from any determination to see the world as it is not. Biblical faith is born from the fact that man's life and history provide us with no hope for justice and peace in this world, except by the power of God. Faith is not a deduction made from our experience of man and nature. It is confidence and hope in God who is neither man nor nature. The believer in God is a confirmed disbeliever in man. What he sees gives him no hope, therefore he believes in Him whom he does not see and hopes for that which is not a fact. His faith does not confuse his sight, nor does his hope neutralize his despair. He sees the dark, and believes in God. He despairs of man and nature, and he clings to God. He is at once a believer and an unbeliever, hopeful and not hopeful, blessed and unhappy. Such is Biblical faith, and such the only faith open to the contemporary man who prefers truth to lies. Christianity is the good news that God is love. Such is its faith. But it also is the bad news that Love is the Crucified. Such is the supreme fact in its history.

2. *The Power of the Cross of Jesus Christ*

There is no more compelling evidence of human folly than the transformation of Christianity into a Cross-less religion. The way in which the piercing tragedy of the crucifixion of a "sinless Man" has been turned into an unfortunate incident in a happy life is a supreme revelation of the obdurate determination of men to be happy rather than live by painful truth. Christians have seldom shown more disingenuous cleverness than in their attempts to "explain" the Cross. Eager to celebrate the love of God, they have passed over as lightly as possible the fact that the Cross reveals the tragedy of life at its darkest and in its insufferable intensity. Jesus of Nazareth died, as a matter of fact, because He was a good man in an evil world. In His suffering and death, the world branded itself as the enemy of righteousness. It has never condemned itself as sinful and murderous more dramatically and unforgettably than in the Cross of Christ. Jesus of Nazareth was a righteous man, and good and respectable people murdered Him. The religious and the wise of this world, the leaders and reformers of the people, the upholders of the Law and the Temple, the custodians of public welfare and order—for fear of loss of their religion and law, their authority and prosperity, their security and life—possessed of the same madness and secularism which underlies all sin, took hold of the Servant of God and nailed Him to the Cross. They found Jesus preaching the Kingdom of God to a hopeless and helpless people, befriending the sinners and publicans, and healing their diseases, teaching them to love their enemies and laboring to mitigate, by word and example, the folly of lust for power and possessions in a doomed world, teaching them sobriety, humility, unaggressiveness, indifference to things men sin in order to secure: they took Him and did away with Him. The Cross of Christ exposed the tragic sinfulness of men in rebellion against God, against their place in the world, against their destiny of weakness and dependence. There is no more frightening, sobering, humiliating, despair-provoking fact in history than the Cross of Christ; no event which is more suited to make us cry in hopeless desperation in our bondage to sin, more convincing evidence of the indifferent cruelty with which righteousness is crucified, and the righteous man, as well as the unrighteous, murdered and destroyed in this world of whoredom and bloodshed. No exhibit of man's baseness and nature's callousness paraded by the atheists is comparable to the Cross. Christianity, the religion of the Cross and the way of the Cross, is rooted in the tragic sense of life, and is silly as well as meaningless without it.

Let us not deceive ourselves. The love of God does not have all its boasted superlative influence upon us unless it is a love which accentuates the tragedy of life. It is revealed in its true power only when it is recognized as the one hope of men in bondage to sin-death. The goodness of God, the mercy of God, the love of God are made manifest in the miracle of a righteous Man's willing death in obedience to God, while sinners rebel against a destiny which their sin makes more than just. We despise the goodness of God and insult the Cross of Christ when we close our hearts and minds to the enormity of our sinful plight and to the wonder of the crucified Son of Man. Let us not deceive ourselves. It is only as we consider our desperate need of God that we believe and hope properly, that we learn of the compassion which led Jesus to the Cross and which remains our one hope of deliverance from man's inhumanity to man. Our vaunted love of God, our gratitude and the consequent desire to honor and serve Him, remain abortive without a most unflinching and earnest view of our common plight in this valley of the shadow of death.

Too easy a "faith" in the love of God is sheer credulity, and as such possesses no magical power to "change lives." We live and remain in sin-death. Nothing but spiritual myopia can alter our vision of this fact. Our faith in the love of God is a cry, a hope, a yearning, born in the midst of real and continuing despair. In this life faith and despair cannot be separated from each other without the former degenerating into a cheap and worthless panacea, and the latter into poison or pretense. It is in their conjunction that truth and goodness have their roots. Despair must remain an integral part of religion, as well as its source. Otherwise the fountains of compassion within us are dried up and we are left with the complacency and ill-concealed pride so characteristic of "religion." When faith destroys despair, it also destroys love, and itself ceases to be faith.

Christian love is inseparable from the Christian Cross, and the latter from the "Christian Epic." The Cross is central to a story which tells of the creation of the world and man by God ("And God saw that it was good."), of the entrance of sin-death into the world, of the many follies and wickednesses of men, of the promises of God to His servants, of the Law which men disobeyed, of the prophets whom men rejected, of new promises, of new sins and sufferings, of despair before the coming of the Promised One, of His coming, ministry, suffering, death and resurrection, of the gift of the Spirit, the founding of the Church, and the watching and waiting for the Kingdom of God where sin-death would be replaced by righteousness-life. This "Christian Epic" is the story of man's ultimate despair and hope. It is the story of the tragedy of man and of the undying hope within him. It, the *whole* of it, not only the happy passages in it, reveals man to himself as a person, as a soul, as "intelligent creation." It is the permanent expression of the conflict within the soul which makes all men brothers one to another, and inspires the compassion which is the cornerstone of the good life.

It is no longer possible to build a Christian ethic upon the "infinite value of human personality," or upon authoritative "teachings of Jesus," or upon an idealism which depends upon "faith in man." A vital ethic for our time cannot be built upon rationalistic and romantic optimism. It has to be an ethic congenial to the contemporary man's sense of his insignificance in the universe, his "realistic" intuition of the limits of human power and goodness, his perceptions of ends and purposes which transcend his comfort and happiness, his gallant if abortive efforts to live with dignity and integrity in a world which denies him ultimate self-realization; an ethic inspired by humility, sobriety, and willingness to become instrumental to ends which transcend the dictates of self-love. An anthropocentric religion is no longer a fitting foundation for a vital ethic. The only alternative to worldliness as the foundation of such an ethic is "theocentric religion," in which the anguish of life is opposed to the knowledge of God, to honoring, obeying and serving God.

The "Reformation theology" is the Christian Epic with emphases which make it peculiarly relevant to the mind and temper of our age. In the quest of a metaphysics for a contemporary ethics, the Protestant's first recourse should be to the religion of the reformers. The Protestant versions of the doctrines of Original Sin, Justification by Faith, Election and Predestination, together with the related emphasis upon the honor of God, are supremely congenial to contemporary insights into man and his place in nature. "Original Sin" is an impressive testimony to Protestantism's awareness of the radical malady of sin-death which circumscribes human life. "Justification by Faith" is the complete repudiation of magic and idoltary in religion, and a single-minded recognition of man's lack of the power to perform the miracle of destroying sin-death. It is the admission that our one Hope is God the Creator. "Election" and Predestination" are witnesses to the ultimate mystery of man's dependence upon the Eternal, to the facts of men's different powers and stations in this world which defy adequate explanation, to the necessity of a dignified acceptance of the "constitution of the world" which is prior to all human wish or will. They are telling expressions of the humility whereby man is willing to let God be God! to accept the prior right of God to make man instrumental to His glory; to find blessedness in God's electing and predestinating one to the end of one's honoring and serving God; to rejoice that *God* knows His last end in creating the world and has not left the humble without knowledge whereby he may live wisely and soberly as befits his creaturehood. "Double Election" and "Double Predestination," together with the related "willingness to be damned to the glory of God," are man's last profession of the priority of God to His creation, and his last confession of the sin generated by self-love. They are the ultimate definitions of the "disinterested love of God" which men pretend but do not possess. They are the scandalous but chastening utterances of that obedience which remains essential to Protestant piety.

3. *Obedience to God and the Service of God*

In the Protestant ethic, as in the Bible, obedience occupies a place of honor among the virtues. It is the first fruit of humility and the measure of our deliverance from rebellion against God. It establishes in practice man's recognition of the primacy of God, of His will and purpose. The obedient man knows himself as confronted with a Will which is prior to his own wish or desire. He is guided by an objective Law which demands his conformity to it, by objective facts which reveal that Law and bend his will to act accordingly. It is his duty to hear, to see, to understand, to submit, to obey, and to act accordingly. He is mindful of his dependence, of his subservience, of his duty, rather than of his freedom, or power, or rights. His mind and heart are dominated by fact and necessity, by causes and consequences, by ends and means, which confront him with an obligation, a task, a choice. Like the historians of the Old Testament, he looks at the past and the present with the purpose of discovering the "constitution" which conditions the course of events. Like its lawgivers, he seeks to learn the will of the Moral Governor concerning the conduct of life. Like its prophets, he sets out to warn himself and others of the consequences of rebellion against God. Like its poets, he sets his heart in motion toward repentance and repeated surrender to the will of God.

Obedience is religion's counterpart to the demand of intelligence that proper regard be paid to facts. It is the call to objectivity which is contrary to self-will, wishful thinking, subjection to desire which can even camouflage itself as conscience. Thus there is a kinship between the contemporary idea that the good life is dependent upon intelligent regard for facts and religion's hoary demand that men obey God. Biblical and Protestant concern with obedience, and contemporary "reverence for facts" belong together as against all clamor for high ideals and noble sentiments which are considered essential to "moral progress." Voluntary obedience to God and not persistent attention to exalting notions about human power and dignity, is the basis of the Protestant ethic. The true saint (as Edwards would say), like any man devoted to truth and reality, be he scientist, artist, or craftsman, is too preoccupied with the object of his attention, to celebrate his freedom and power to attend to it. The Protestant's mind and heart are turned towards God. Hence any virtue he may exercise is either done unconsciously or recognized as the work of an unprofitable servant. Were there more religion, more love of truth and beauty, there would be less of abortive celebration of love and devotion and all the rest, less self-conscious preoccupation with our freedom to love and excellence in loving. Contemporary religion, with its constant concern with the powers and virtues of man, is touching evidence of moral and intellectual bewilderment in our day. It is as clumsy and ineffective as a poor athlete worrying about his muscles or a baffled scientist worrying about his eyes and mind. Man's proper power and freedom is proportionate to his devotion to truth and to his obedience to its dictates. The athlete had better attend to his goal, the scientist to his problem, the religious man to his God.

The knowledge of God, the love of God, obedience to God—the service of God. The service of God is the ultimate demand of the Protestant ethic. Man's service is essentially his act of obedience. It is his behavior in consequence of his assent to the will of God as revealed in what God does and demands. Here also, attention to an objective realm of facts, displaying the Divine glory, is necessary. The service of God is none other than the glorifying of God in conduct. It is man's alignment of himself with the purpose of God as revealed in nature and history. It is the practical aspect of that devotion to understanding "the order and connection of things" which is essential to knowing and honoring God. "Service" seals Protestantism as a theocentric religion, and consists of practice based upon an affirmation of the ultimate priority of God and His glory as displayed in the world of men and things. In serving God, we acknowledge Him as the *alpha* and *omega* of creation.

But here also, if we are to go beyond pious gesture, we have to see that the service of God is inseparable from that temper of heart-mind which turns us to the world of facts with the intention of seeing and understanding in a perspective in which *we* are not central, in which no creature in heaven or on earth is central. The true service of God is rooted in the disposition to refuse absolute loyalty to *anything*—to religion, science, art, or business; to the Church, the state, or the nation; to race, class, family, friend, or one's own self. It is grounded in that sense of vanity which destroys the pretense of things noblest and dearest to divine claim and authority upon us, in that compassionate sense of proportion which demands the love of any creature as creature first and according to its special nature second.

To think of the service of God in analogy to human relations is often dangerous and misleading. We cannot serve God as we serve men because God is God and not man, the Creator and not a creature. We serve God as an act of obedience; whereas we serve our fellow men as we obey God's will concerning us and them. We do not co-operate with God as we do with our fellow men. We co-operate with God by making His will our own, by receiving His grace in our justification; whereas we co-operate with men as we add our powers to their own. We do not help God as we help our fellow men. We "help God" when He uses us to accomplish His will; whereas we help our fellow men as we fulfil their needs. We serve God, co-operate with His creation, help *ourselves.*

Some aspect of God's glory becomes manifest whether we obey Him or do not. We cannot act against the will of God and flout His purposes. All things are and will be to the glory of God. When we fail to learn His will and to serve Him, we suffer, not God whose glory is revealed even in our suffering. Hence, there should be less of this folly and presumption of men's setting themselves to add their virtue and power to "the perfections of God." It is indeed amazing generosity for sinning and dying men to supplement the glory of God, how much more amazing than that we should propose to help the sun run its course and shine upon the good and the evil. God needs our service only in the sense that we need to understand and obey Him. Is God's sin to be blotted out? Is His death to be overcome? Is His eternity to be safeguarded? Is His glory to be burnished? It is difficult to find a more striking evidence of human disingenuousness than the perversion of the service of God to helping God. And the Protestant antidote to such folly is the unitedness of obedience and service in our religion. Men who obey do not help or assist; they listen and do what they are told. *God* helps those who understand Him and obey, as nature helps those who understand causes and effects and act accordingly.

We must not fall into the trap of conceiving of the

service of God too closely after the analogy of our relationship to nature. Religion is not "science." The service of God is the consequence of that obedience which is born of the "anguish of life" within us. The God-centeredness of the service of God is the virtual solution of the problem of destiny which nonetheless persists and embarrasses our obedience. Religious objectivity is attained in the midst of single-minded and thoroughgoing subjectivity. Only the man who knows the despair of rebellion against his destiny of sin-death knows the peace and joy of obedience to God and of the service of God.

In Protestant religion, the conception of the service of God has been inspired partly by aversion to the "contemplative life" which is the crown of Catholic piety. It has also led to a "practical Christianity" which has opposed itself to the historic otherworldliness of Christianity, both Protestant and Catholic. The results of such antagonism to otherworldly contemplation and to contemplation itself have been gravely detrimental to the service of God. Calvinism, bent upon serving God according to scriptural precept, produced much legalism, fanaticism, and tyranny of the respectable and powerful. It became a tool of a *bourgeoisie* whose interests demanded virtues like honesty and industry which were necessary to maximum prosperity and an undisturbed possession of worldly goods. The custodians of God's justice and vengeance ruled towns, villages and families with an iron hand, and often lost all sense of understanding and compassion. Thus an authoritarian and legalistic conception of God's will was combined with the will to dominate; "charity" was opposed to justice and "the service of God," and became a higher virtue to be exercised only when the authority of God's vice-regents was safe. From the very first, Reformed Protestantism, depending upon direct and obvious knowledge of God's will given in the Bible, has been lacking in the humility and charity which are necessary for mitigating man's ubiquitous inhumanity to man. A noncontemplative Calvinism produced much callousness and suffering, and made the service of God a terrifying affair.

In our own day, in a still noncontemplative Protestantism, the service of God has become a "simple goodness" whereby men of goodwill seek to better the lot of their fellow men. The old stiffness and severity are gone. But the ghosts of the old legalism and authoritarianism, a sense of direct access to the Divine will through the letter of the Bible and naïve certainty about things good and bad, a now genteel intolerance of nonconformers, and a steady desire to reform others and to bring them into line—in short moralism justified by the Bible—are still with us. Thus a simple-minded, goodhearted and busybody Protestantism continues in the simple and yet strangely ineffective practice of the "service of God" or rather the service of men. With the ideal of maximum common happiness in their minds, naïve enthusiasm in their hearts, and excerpts from the Bible in their hands, many Protestants have gone forth to fight the evils of the day, swinging left and right, hitting and missing at random, hoping and wishing vigorously, always exhorting, protesting, and surprised at public inertia and resistance to their efforts. Amazing activity, amazing failure. One can hardly resist the thought that Protestantism is "beating around the bush," leaving undone "the one thing needful," wasting itself in chasing phantoms and quixotic blustering.

4. *Contemplation and Criticism in the Protestant Life*

It is time that Protestant thought should cultivate more discernment and quiet, humble wisdom in its treatment of contemporary sin and evil. We need desperately a species of contemplation which will give us more insight, patience, and that charity which shall enable us to understand each other, to bear with dignity our common burden of sin and suffering, to mitigate our callousness, to decrease our power to cause pain, and to counteract our injustices with a decent forgetfulness of our rights to "life and the pursuit of happiness"; which will give us a little sense of proportion, a little dose of doubt and self-criticism, a grain of dissatisfaction with our high-minded censoriousness and lack of feeling for those we consider sinners in our midst; enough self-knowledge to help us attend to our own folly and sin, enough humility to keep us from herding together and shouting against other people's sins, enough wisdom to repent of our own sins and to eat our daily bread praying for Divine forgiveness. Then, maybe, the wise and gracious God would bless the work of our hands and turn it into good. We could do much good by becoming less harmful.

Protestant contemplation cannot be a simple matter of reversion to Catholic piety. Catholic otherworldliness and spirituality are too belief-full, visionary, and complacent for the contemporary man who has not been brought up to take the mythology of angelic hosts and mediating saints for granted. Protestant religiosity must be more agnostic, more disturbed, more despairing, more humble about its power and virtue; it must be a religion of hope and trust, and nevertheless a religion of prayer to Him who is neither man nor anything man makes or possesses. Catholic piety is rooted in unquestioning faith in the Church, in its teaching, cult, and commandments. Protestant piety is rooted in the unflinching perception of man's need for God. The former is a confirmed optimism based upon the doctrine of a divine Church; the latter is trust in God's Word spoken in the Bible, intensifying man's despair as well as challenging it to seek first the Kingdom of God. The basic doctrine of Catholicism is that of the Incarnation, which is the ground for its sacramentalism and legalism, for its certainty that it possesses the Way and the Truth. The basic doctrine of Protestantism is that of the Atonement which points to the Cross as the symbol of human life in this world and declares the vanity of all ways and truths except the Way and the Truth of God revealed upon the Cross. The Catholic has peace knowing that he is under the protecting and guiding care of the Church and of its hierarchy. The peace of the Protestant is in clinging to God in Christ the crucified and risen, to God's Word that His power and righteousness are sufficient against sin and death; it is the peace of those whose spirits rejoice in God's righteousness and in God's eternity. The ideal of Catholic contemplation is the "vision of God" in which all contradictions are resolved, all evils overcome, all suffering eliminated. Protestant contemplation is inspired at all times by the anguish of life in this world of sin-death, and by trust in God and concern with the glory of God revealed in nature and history and above all in Jesus Christ. Protestant piety is never without the tensions between time and eternity, life and death, the love of self and the love of God, concern with worldly goods and the sense of their vanity, faith and despair, and sin and righteousness. Its peculiar ethic is born of these tensions. Its present task is to be true to itself and to be worthy of the peculiar treasure entrusted to it. It is the conviction of the present writer, as stated and argued throughout this essay, that a Protestantism mindful of its own genius and devoted to its own calling will, by the grace of God, be a leaven of charity and justice in the vast lump of contemporary sin.

In the meanwhile, God must be served, practically and in detail. While we contemplate our need for God and His righteousness, we have to live facing the problems of the day. Our religion offers no ready-made answers to the problems of justice and peace as these appear in our time. Hence as we pray we must also work with the thousand intricate problems produced by our overintricate age. The religious man has no short cut to Utopia. He must *know* the immediate and proximate causes of the evils around him and including him. He must weigh facts and see reasons, consider ends and their means, struggle with particular impediments and devise particular methods of procedure. Religion is not a substitute for knowledge, intellectual responsibility, proper decision and action. The religious man, whatever his moral, economic and political convictions, must know and think as well as feel and act.

Religion is essential for right thinking and acting. Its function, in its direct application to particular problems, is to produce and encourage that objectivity which is difficult and rare. It is the duty of religion to introduce new perspectives for vision and thought, and therefore for action; to insinuate into us that disinterestedness and impartiality which much thinking pretends but seldom achieves; to open the eyes of the people to the discrepancies between their professions and their behavior, and to minimize the pretensions and hypocrisy which accompany our efforts at rationality and understanding; to illumine minds blinded by self-interest and to set free wills in bondage to fear-full self-love.

Original Sin, according to the Protestant view, involves *total* depravity, the corruption of reason as well as of the heart. The sinner's reason is under the domination of fear. Hence life is perverted to egoism, and reason becomes the instrument of aggression and domination. One sees others from a perspective in which one's self is the center of the world, and makes all goods to converge toward one's own good. One contemplates all goods in relation to the objective of personal happiness, and thus replaces the world of a multiplicity of ends with an illusory world of a series of personal ends. Given these ends, reason degenerates into the craftiness necessary to attain them. The reasoning of a sinner may be clever and effective, but it is always twisted and erroneous, nourishing itself with the lie that his self and his goods have a peculiar and unique significance in this our common world. Thus the effort of the mind to understand is doomed to failure from the very start. The things and persons around us, with their private histories—with their own feelings and ends—are placed in a false and arbitrary perspective. We are cut off from the position of an impartial observer. Objectivity becomes impossible, and therewith true knowledge is eliminated. Sin condemns the mind to the love and satisfied contemplation of falsehood.

Such prostitution of reason has profound influence upon the more subtle business of understanding which involves the heart. It produces a rationality which operates with the doctrine that man's first duty is to himself; which regards all facts unrelated to self-love as "cold and hard." It produces a "realistic," "business-like," "unsentimental" mind which glories in overlooking the feelings of others and pretends that our neighbor is not a man. It impersonalizes people, ignores their private existence, reduces them to tools, and thus destroys the seeds of justice and mercy in the human soul.

A religion cognizant of the depravity of human reason would contribute fundamentally to the problem of right thinking in our day. It cannot displace psychology, sociology, economics, etc., and can ill afford to neglect the facts they disclose. But it can become a potent instrument of criticism and can convict experts in these fields of knowledge of prejudices and presumptions which make their cogitations ineffective in the struggle for justice and peace. It can show that reason in bondage to self-interest cannot, in the nature of the case, solve the ethical problems confronting it. The impotence of the nonreligious mind, however sharp and well-informed, in the face of the recurrent crises of our time, its inability to do any more than to postpone the days of reckoning, is a terrible fact pointing to a fundamental corruption of reason rooted in self-consciousness. To expose the folly and bondage of sinful reason, to encourage a genuine objectivity in which the multiplicity of souls in our world is recognized as a fact of supreme importance, to discipline the mind to be permanently critical of its reasoning and judgments—these are indispensable tasks of a religion aware of the continued frustration caused by the sin which is in our minds as well as in our hearts. The corruption of the mind by self-centeredness is a ubiquitous fact. And it is the function of religion which is aware of the basis of self-centeredness in a perverted anguish of life, to increase the mind's integrity and to restore it to its high function as an instrument for the discovery of truth. A Protestantism which ignores its duty towards the cleansing of the mind is doomed to do poor service to this our age of bewilderment and helplessness before demonic forces which are leading us to ruin. On the other hand, a Protestantism which exposes the sin within us and teaches us radical self-criticism, which leads us to the fear of God and concern for the glory of God, will act as a true Church of God and become a genuine power toward peace and righteousness among men. A Protestantism with its heart and mind set upon honoring and serving God will not only make itself worthy of its heritage but will also receive new strength for its ministry to the needs of this generation. It may not destroy the latter's sin and suffering; but it will sow in it seeds of wisdom and charity to which God will give the increase hundredfold: in His proper time and to His greater glory.

Instead of a Bibliography

The first chapter of this book was written under the influence of Luther's commentaries on *Romans* and *Galatians, Living Philosophies* (Simon and Schuster, 1931), and personal impressions of contemporary Protestant religion. The second chapter was inspired by the conflict between popular and prophetic religion in ancient Israel, by Calvinistic religion as exemplified by John Calvin and Jonathan Edwards, and by contemporary attempts at a "disinterested love of God" as seen in the writings of Irwin Edman, James Thurber, A. N. Whitehead, George Santayana, Lin Yutang, Walter Lippmann, etc. In spite of the fact that these men differ one from another in important and various respects, they all give expression to the deep-seated conviction of the contemporary man that man is neither the center nor the "last end" of the universe. I cannot produce a bibliography for the third chapter. It contains my reflections on the relation of sin to death, a singularly neglected topic in Western theology and ethics. The forthright classic statement that death entered into the world through the sin of Adam is, I think, unsatisfactory. For my views on the nature of "social sin," I am deeply indebted to Reinhold Niebuhr. Karl Barth's *The Word of God and the Word of Man* initiated me into my present understanding of the Biblical mind. As for my views on "the Protestant life," I can only hope that they are Biblical, Reformed, and fairly intelligent.